Prehistoric Slavic Contraction

Jiří Marvan

Prehistoric Slavic Contraction

translated by *Wilson Gray*

Library of Congress Cataloging in Publication Data

Marvan, Jiří.
   Prehistoric Slavic contraction.

   Translated from the Czech.
   Bibliography: p. 171.
   Includes indexes.
   1. Slavic languages — Contraction. 2. Slavic
languages — Phonology, Historical. 3. Proto-Slavic
language — Phonology, Historical. I. Title.
PG77.M313   891.8   78-23498
ISBN 0-271-00210-7

PREFACE

The purpose of this monograph is to outline the origin and process of contraction as it took place in the proto-dialects of the future Czech, Sorbian, Polish, Slovak, Slovenian and Serbo-Croatian languages in about the 9th to 11th centuries. While some attention is paid to the Slavic territory adjacent to the East — that is, to the future Ukrainian and Bulgarian/Macedonian dialects — the dialects of the two extreme areas in the East and the West have been treated in separate publications: Russian in 1973[1] and Polabian in 1977.[2]

Our conception differs from the traditional attitude to the available data mainly in the assumption that the discriminative treatment of contraction by different proto-dialects is not a handicap but rather an efficient and safe means of reconstructing territorial, chronological and structural stratification. This factor establishes the territory of contraction, with the focus in Czech, probably including West Slovak; the central region in surrounding proto-dialects of Upper Sorbian, South Polish, East Slovak, North Slovenian, Čakavian; the periphery in more remote proto-dialects of the same "future languages," i.e. in Lower Sorbian, North Polish, Central Slovak, South Slovenian, Štokavian; and the transperiphery in the neighboring Ukrainian and Bulgarian/Macedonian proto-dialects.

Further, this factor replaces a "flat," one-level description of contraction with a conception of a process consisting of several (six) consecutive stages. First of all, however, this factor provides the ground for an attempt to correlate these chronological

---

1. See "Russkoe stjaženie i slavjanskaja doistoričeskaja kontrakcija," in *Melbourne Slavonic Studies 8,* pp. 5-9. The article contends that, should the connection between these two processes be established, the contraction would be the most important Slavic change stretching across 2000 km and 1000 years.

2. See "Kontraktion und Prosodie im Polabischen und ihr westslavischer Kontext," in *Zeitschrift für slavische Philologie XXXIX,* pp. 373-383. This study demonstrates that the prehistoric contraction spread to Polabian and yielded results which are remarkably similar to those in some Polish, Slovak and Slovenian dialects.

stages with the increasingly deeper language strata, making feasible an assumption that the prehistory of language, both as an objective entity and as our corresponding "model," has its own deep structure which, in its turn, also can be constructed.

This book is an open and initial enterprise containing many gaps which can be filled only by efforts of dialectologists and historians of all Slavic languages. We can, for example, assume that very fresh and useful information will be obtained from investigation of contemporary Polish-Ukrainian, North-South Slovenian and Čakavian/Štokavian-Bulgarian/Macedonian border areas concealing isoglosses dating back some 800 to 1000 years.

The author will feel this monograph has fulfilled its purpose if it is treated not as completed research but rather as a modest opening of enquiry into the vast and exciting subject of prehistoric Slavic contraction.

ACKNOWLEDGMENTS

This volume is a translation by Wilson Gray of my manuscript written in Czech. Mr. Gray, a former student of mine, completed the translation with the financial support of the University of California at Davis, to which we both are indebted. He did an excellent job.

The book never would have appeared without the assistance of my Australian friends. Dr. P. Cubberly (Melbourne University) and Mr. Mark Garner (Rusden College) edited the text and compiled the indices. My very special thanks go to Mrs. N. M. Christensen (Melbourne University), for her warm encouragement and practical support. I also acknowledge the outstanding effort of Mr. M. Beissmann, who was responsible for typesetting the book, and of Mrs. J. Kuligowska, who took care of its internal design. The author takes full responsibility for any errors which may remain.

All my family — my wife, Elishka, and my children, Elinka and Thomas — earned my gratitude by sharing my trust in the value of this work.

The author is indebted to a number of Czech, Swedish, American and Australian colleagues, named and unnamed, for their encouragement and help, which permitted him to believe that this volume deserved the time and effort invested.

My late colleague Professor F. Holling (Portland State University) undertook a translation of my book that was not published for reasons beyond his control or mine. The present completed work stands in part as a token of our warm friendship.

TABLE OF CONTENTS

Prehistoric Slavic Contraction

PART ONE

THE PLACE OF CONTRACTION
IN THE SYSTEM OF ISOGLOSSES

CHAPTER I

CHARACTERISTICS OF THE SYSTEM
OF DYNAMIC ISOGLOSSES

1. GENERAL CHARACTERISTICS OF DYNAMIC ISOGLOSSES

1.0 The system of isoglosses is of crucial importance in solving the problems of a proto-language, and consequently, also of the Proto-Slavic language. Provided that the isoglosses cover an entire territory in a coherent manner, we speak of linguistic unity, of a uniform proto-language. If, however, they lose this property, we speak of loss of this unity.

1.1 As follows from this formulation, in the investigation of a proto-language and its disintegration we are concerning ourselves with the development of a system — a compact or a disjunctive system — and thus, in this connection, with dynamic isoglosses or, traditionally, with changes.

1.2 The set of Proto-Slavic changes can be characterized not only chronologically and territorially but also typologically, that is, according to structural type. Though this last method is not intended to displace approaches hitherto in vogue, it nevertheless has the advantage of employing certain objective criteria.

1.2.1 Chronological description in particular can sometimes be rather arbitrary in the investigation of prehistory — such as in applying unconfirmed, often contradictory hypotheses, nor is territorial description necessarily free of problems. Such is the case, for example, regarding epenthetic *l*.

1.2.2 The difficulties in this instance would increase still further, if, for example, Bulgarian were attested only from the same period as the West Slavic languages, so that the later process of the disappearance of this *l* fell into the prehistoric period in South Slavic as well as in West Slavic (cf. Mirčev 1963, 136). However, according to Horálek 1962, 105, fn. 50, not even in the case of Bulgarian have doubts about this element been entirely eliminated. Compare also Bernštejn 1961, where the skeptical views of Mladenov are quoted.

1.3 The advantages of typological characterization lie in the application of the internal, organic criteria which are implied by this approach.

Generally speaking, one may symbolize a dynamic isogloss, an indication of linguistic change, by the formula

$$A \rightarrow B \tag{1!}$$

and formulate it in this manner: Segment A is rewritten as segment B.

As a rule, the symbol $>$ designates a process of change. We shall reserve this symbol for the designation of concrete changes exclusively, e.g. $a > o$, **medŭs > medъ > med** 'honey' etc. We shall not use the symbol * for reconstructed segments, inasmuch as they will form the major topic of discussion. We shall reserve this symbol for hypothetical cases under consideration that are, in point of fact, impossible. The symbol $\Rightarrow$ means "implies".

A we shall term the starting point of a process (input), B its end point (output), — the process itself, or procedent.

Expression (1!) is a general expression for several realizations:

(1) $B = A$; we shall designate this isogloss, which depends upon an identity of end point and starting point, by the expression (for N indicating 'no change')

$$A \rightarrow N \tag{1.1}$$

and term it the STABLE ISOGLOSS. Example: $e > e$.

(2) $B = A$, $B^o = B$, where B designates the sole possible outcome over an entire territory, so that according to (1!)

$$A \rightarrow B^o \tag{1.2}$$

This isogloss we shall term a COMPACT ISOGLOSS. Example: $i > ь$.

(3) $B = A$, $B = B^o$; in this case, B has several territorially differentiated variants which we shall designate by $B^o = B(n)$, so that the whole change, according to (1!), has the form

$$A \rightarrow B(n) \tag{1.3}$$

If we designate the separate territorial variants by the symbols $B^1, B^2, \ldots, B^n$, then by the term $B(n)$ we mean the set of these variants. Example: $tj > č, c, ć, št \ldots$

This isogloss we term a NON-COMPACT ISOGLOSS.

(4) B $=$ A, Bm $=$ N, Where Bm designates a member of the set B(n), i.e. $1 \geqq m \geqq n$. This phenomenon, empirically consistent, has two distinct systemic realizations.

(4a) The segment B^m, not only on the surface, but also in the deep structure, belongs to the set B(n). That is, N is, in the final analysis, in essence an equivalent outcome, so that it holds good that

$$A - B^1 \ldots N \ldots B^n \qquad (1.3')$$

where the term in the position of the outcome represents the set B(n). Thus the entire change (1.3') is merely a variant of the change (1.3). An example of such a change as we shall demonstrate in I/4, is *tl* $>$ *tl, kl, l*.

(4b) The segment Bm does not systemically belong to the set B(n), i.e., the isogloss has not diffused itself over part of an area, so that the whole process has the form

$$\text{I. } A \Rightarrow B$$
$$\text{II. } A \Rightarrow N \qquad (1.4)$$

As an example of such a process we may take denasalization, which did not penetrate into Polish, nor, in part, into other e.g. Macedonian dialects. This isogloss we term DISJUNCTIVE.

Failure to take into consideration this systemic duality can lead to considerable misunderstanding.

1.4 Let us consider some properties of individual isoglosses.

(1) Cases of the type (1.1) are specified as the "conservation" of a particular state as "trivial" isoglosses that cannot give positive evidence of the character of development in a particular linguistic territory. But this conservation may be connected with changes in structure — cf., e.g., case (1.3') — and thus need not be *a priori* irrelevant for the development of structure. Not only change, but also its absence, must be investigated in relation to the system to which it belongs.

(2) Cases of the type (1.2) are considered to be an indication of territorial unity. Such a change is referred to as an isogloss. If there be no such changes, it is accepted that there is no unity.

(3) Cases of the type (1.3) are, on the contrary, considered to be an indication of the disintegration of territorial unity, e.g.

in Shevelov 1964, 608 ff., in Bernštejn 1961, 49 ff. On the surface, this is fully justified. Difficulties arise when, after those that have come about as a consequence of disintegration, compact changes, indicators of continued unity, appear.

1.5   For these reasons a purely "surface" formulation of unity and disintegration is manifestly inadequate. That is to say, every unity, as a result of its development, in addition to producing integrating tendencies, quite regularly produces disintegrating tendencies too. It is unacceptable to consider the disintegration of unity, an inseparable component of every linguistic development, and hence also an indispensable attribute of proto-language, to be necessarily followed by the language breakup, for this would mean that every development of unity simultaneously implies the beginning of disunity. Disintegration may, but need not, lead to breakup. It is, however, always a feature of unity, whether compact or breaking up.

The replacement of "surface" formulation naturally presupposes a new interpretation, chiefly a differentiated interpretation of the results in set $B(n)$. The fact that we have been able to determine the set of $B(n)$ by means of a relatively simple procedure points to its homogeneous character. This uniformity is explained by its common starting point. All of the more important disintegrational changes in Proto-Slavic may be expressed in principle by formula (1.3), which means that not only the starting point, i.e. the object of the change, but also the conditions that motivate the change and the process itself remain in principle unified. The difference is only in the result, in the realization. We are dealing, therefore, with uniformity of content and differentiation of the realization of that uniform content. On the surface the difference is significant, and this method of observation may have its own cognitive value. However, if we concern ourselves with the essence of the change, we must first of all look at its underlying content, and this is uniform.

2.   APPLICATION — INTRODUCTORY REMARKS

2.0   As an example of the above concept of changes we shall put into evidence its application to the problem of the complex development of two-consonant clusters in Proto-Slavic.

2.1   Consonant clusters in that period of Proto-Slavic when

they had not yet undergone any changes, we shall term poly-
phones, and we shall designate each polyphone by the symbol Φ.
The individual consonants that are the components of the polyphone are designated by φ. A polyphone of two components is
designated by Φ2, where the index denotes the number of components, and is called a biphone. Its individual components are
designated by χ, ψ, where the alphabetic order indictes the
order of components in the original polyphone. In general, therefore, the biphone may be expressed as Φ2 $= (χ, ψ)$, with the
provision that a consonant should not stand immediately before
or after it. We have chosen biphones as an example because there
remain unresolved two interesting problems concerning them:
epenthetic *l* and the development of the biphones *dl, tl.*

2.2 For the determination of the relationships of the components in biphones, we shall classify the components according
to two distinctive features: continuantness (fricativeness) vs. non-
continuantness (plosiveness) (hereafter f:p) and non-sonorant-
ness (true-consonantness) vs. sonorantness (C:S), as in table 1.

	f	p
C	*s, z, x*	*k, g, p, b, t, d*
S	*r, l, w, j*	*n, m*

TABLE 1

We shall symbolize here the velar fricative **ch** by the (Cyrillic) letter **x.**
By the symbols **C, S,** we shall refer to those components having the
corresponding property, by a combination of these symbols to those components having both corresponding properties. E.g., Cf will denote a
non-sonorant fricative, i.e., **s, z, x.** By the symbol / we shall denote
"either/or": a/b "either a or b"; by the symbol //, we shall denote
"both//and": a//b "both a and b". The symbol N means "no change".

2.3 The rules:

(0) Priority rule: the rules are ordered disjunctively, i.e., if
two rules may apply to the same case, then the earlier rule will
apply and the later rule will not apply.

(1) The rule of regressive assimilation of voicing for row C,
i.e., for cases where $χ//ψ = C$:

$$ψ^v \rightarrow (χ, ψ)^v$$

where v indicates voiced/unvoiced C feature.

A. Cases where $\chi = \psi$

   (2)   *tt* > *st, dd* > *zd*

   (3) $(\chi, \psi) \rightarrow$ φ, i.e., $\chi//\psi$

B. Cases where $\chi \neq \psi$

   (4)   *(kt)'* > *tj*

   (5) $\psi = j \Rightarrow (\chi, \psi) \rightarrow \chi'; \chi' \cong \chi$, cf. **I/3**

   (6)   for $\chi/\psi = w$

  (6a) *wr-, wl-* > *r, l* (in initial position)

  (6b) *bw* > *w*

  (6c) $\psi = w \Rightarrow (\chi, \psi) \rightarrow$ N

   (7) $\chi = S \Rightarrow (\chi, \psi) \rightarrow$ N (because an S forms a diphthong with a preceding vowel)

   (8)   *sr, zr* > *str, zdr*

   (9) $\psi = r \Rightarrow (\chi, \psi) \rightarrow$ N

 (10) $\chi = Cf \Rightarrow (\chi, \psi) \rightarrow$ N

 (11) *pt* > *st/t*

 (12) $\psi = C \Rightarrow (\chi, \psi) \rightarrow \psi$

Case (5), which also involves the problem of the development of epenthetic *l*, deserves special analysis. In other respects all cases are exhausted by these rules, except for those cases where $\psi = S$, which are not considered above under (6b), (6c), (8), (9). Rule (5) and the uninvestigated cases where $\psi = S$ (the biphones *tl, dl*) will be the subject of the following paragraphs.

3. THE DEVELOPMENT OF TWO-CONSONANT CLUSTERS WITH *j* AS THE SECOND COMPONENT

3.1 Rule (5) from Section 2 may be formulated thus: A consonant fuses with a following *j*, by which it is qualitatively modified. This has the following results:

(1) An S that is non-labial becomes palatal: *rj* > *ŕ, lj* > *l' nj* > *ń*.

(2) For a Cf a change into a hushing sibilant generally occurs: *sj//xj* > *š, zj* > *ž*.

(3) For a Ce we shall assume the same motivated development as in the preceding cases. Provided that we leave aside the particular cases to be resolved here, affrication generally occurs: *kj* > *č, gj* > *ž; tj* > *č, ć, c, št* and *dj* > *(d)ž, dz, (d)z, žd*.

The explanation of epenthetic *l* is obvious in this system. The remaining Ce, i.e., *p, b,* under these conditions were affricated in the same manner. The fricative element here was none other than epenthetic *l.*

For Ce it is consequently possible to stipulate a general change of affrication.

3.2 From 3.1 one can draw the following conclusions:

(1) The rise of epenthetic *l* is an outcome of the affrication of *p, b;* this kind of affrication is only a concrete form of the general affrication valid for all Ce. The formations *pl' bl'* are hence single, indivisible speech-sounds, cf. Bernštejn 1961, 170: "ne-členimaja v fonetičeskom otnošeniji jedinica" (phonetically indivisible unit).

(2) The rise of epenthetic *l* from the standpoint of the system is shown to be a process that involves the whole of Slavic territory, cf. on this e.g., Komárek 1962, 39 ff., with literature.

(3) It is necessary to comprehend the rise of epenthetic *l* in conjunction with labial sonorants, i.e., *m, w,* as a secondary morphological process, analogous to Russian *grafl'u.* It remains a question whether epenthetic *l* after these sounds exists in the root at all.

3.3 For this interpretation of the development of Ce, it is not in principle necessary to reconstruct the intermediate developmental stages between a given starting point and its outcome. If it is done thus, cf., e.g., Bernštejn 1961, 166 ff., then, indeed, it can have, with the proper approach, a bearing on the comparison of development in Slavic and Baltic. However, it does not say much about the phonological development of Slavic itself, cf. ibid., 166. Several such hypotheses, investigated as a system, lead to notions of far reaching changes in the system, changes about which we can nevertheless know nothing. Thus, the assumption that Ce reached affrication via a stage of palatals, i.e., *k, g, t, d, p, b,* sometimes also via a stage of long palatals, as, e.g., in Bernštejn, loc. cit., leads to the assumption that, as Horálek 1962, 105, states rather skeptically, "Common Slavic had a rather well-developed binary opposition of softness in paired consonants". But this is, in the absence of any supporting evidence whatever, and overly free explanation of the surface data.

3.4 The hypothesis concerning the palatalization of Ce apparently rests on an assumption of Balto-Slavic unity. But in

Proto-Baltic as a whole, not simply in Proto-East-Baltic alone, the situation is anything but clear, cf. Stang 1966, 101 ff. Examples like Lith. *sj* > *ś*, but Prus. and Ltv. *sj* > *š*, would indicate that not even Baltic itself was uniform in the development of binary opposition of softness in paired consonants. The Prus. form *wargien* "copper" (cf. op. cit., 106), but Lith. *varis*, gen. *vario*, i.e., [*varo*], could mean that in certain cases a fusion of *j* with a preceding consonant did not occur in Prus. at all.

On the same basis we can now reject the claim that Lithuanian, which carried out the affriction of *tj, dj*, lacks epenthetic *l*. Lithuanian carried out affrication not in the system Ce, but only in these two consonants, without thereby violating the principle of a paired binary opposition in softness. In Latvian, this principle is still continually losing ground: Ce, perhaps not entirely unconnected with this, is subject to affrication as a consequence (cf. Ltv. palatalization of the type *dzīvs* as against Lth. *gývas*), and epenthetic *l* also appears, cf. Slavic *pl'uti*, Ltv. *spĺaut*, Lith. *spiauti*.

3.5 These skeptical comments in no way preclude the common reconstruction of Slavic and Baltic processes. On the contrary, a systemic approach can only contribute to the investigation of their relationship. Thus, the series of rules in 2.3 is valid also for Baltic, and could have been formulated for the entire Balto-Slavic area. This is the situation, for example, as concerns rules 1, 2, 3, 6, 7 (including note), and 9. Here Slavic could possibly repay, at least a little, its debt in the reconstruction of Baltic. Comparison with Baltic could, on the other hand, define the series of rules with greater precision and give them greater chronological accuracy in their sequence (chronology has been taken into consideration to some extent in the postulation of rule 0, i.e., the rule for the ordering of the rules). This undoubtedly worthwhile task is, however, beyond the scope of this study.

4. THE DEVELOPMENT OF CLUSTERS WITH A SONORANT AS SECOND COMPONENT

4.1 We consider cases where χ = Ce; ψ = *l, n, m*, so that it concerns biphones and their development:

χ ╲ ψ	k, g	p, b	t, d
l	−	−	(!)
n	−	+	+
m	0	+	+

TABLE 2

Explanatory notes:
+ indicates $(\chi, \psi) \rightarrow$ ψ (monophonization)
− indicates $(\chi, \psi) \rightarrow$ N
0 indicates that a biphone is not known to the system
(!) indicates the biphones *tl, dl*

Phonemes differing only in voicing undergo the same changes. Therefore, if there is at least one of a pair of biphones differing only in this
feature, we hold as known both members of the pair (e.g., **bm⟩ m** ⇒
pm⟩ m) or, more simply, the whole pair (i.e., **bm⟩ m** ⇒ **bm//pm ⟩ m**).

4.2   The components in the first row and in the first
column in table 2 clearly differ in their "tolerance", i.e., in their
ability to preserve the biphone without change to realize a stable
isogloss. In contrast to this, the remaining components support
monophonization. We shall call the latter ones "dominants"
(symbol D), and the former "tolerant" components (*l, k, g*)
"subdominants" (symbol d).

4.3   The primary rule, i.e., the rule realized simultaneously
with the rules in 2.3, reads: A biphone is subject to change
only if both components are dominants, or specifically,

$\chi//\psi = D \Rightarrow (\chi, \psi) \rightarrow$ ψ and, consequently a biphone
does not change if at least one component is a subdominant, i.e.

$\chi/\psi/(\chi//\psi) = d \Rightarrow (\chi, \psi) \rightarrow$ N.

Therefore, it would be possible to supplement the rules in
2.3 thus: To rule 9 add ψ = *l*, so that this rule would read:
9. ψ = Sf ⇒ (χ ψ) → N. Further, introduce these rules:

13. χ = Cv ⇒ (χ, ψ) → N
14. χ = Cv', ψ = e ⇒ (χ, ψ) → N,

where Cv indicates a velar Ce and Cv' a non-velar Ce. Table 2a
thus has the following form:

χ ʎ'	k, g	p, b	t, d
l	−	−	−
n	−	+	+
m	−	+	+

TABLE 2a

Thus the system develops entirely regularly in the West Slavic languages.

4.4 The absence of the pairs of biphones *km, gm,* played a decisive part in the deformation of this system in the remaining Slavic languages, i.e., in the remaining Slavic territory. Even if it appeared that these biphones would be structurally permissible as an outcome, cf. 4.3, their material absence operated so that it could be interpreted as a consequence of monophonization. That is why, for example, there is in Old Church Slavic *didragъma* (cf. Horálek 1962, 111) where ъ, which separates *g* and *m,* signals the non-existence of a cluster of two consonants.

In languages of this type, where a 0 in an boundary position (in Table 2) is treated as a +, the status of the boundary position is, entirely symmetrically, likewise changed from (!) into +, so that the system assumes a new balanced shape:

	k, g	p, b	t, d
l	−	−	+
n	−	+	+
m	+	+	+

TABLE 2b

4.5 It is worth noting that in the entire Slavic territory, i.e., in all three Slavic areas, but independently of one another, there occurred a local change of *tl, dl* to *kl, gl,* cf., e.g., Bernštejn 1961, 190 ff. This very territorial distribution of the phenomenon shows that no doubt a specific, yet nevertheless, patent manifestation of unity is involved. The parallelism of this process in a series of territorially independent areas indicates the identity of structural conditions. The problem is their interpretation.

This process represents a compromise between the state in 4.3 (*tl, dl* > N) and the state in 4.4 (*tl, dl* > *l*), cf. the pertinent tables, 2a, 2b. The compromise is realized so that state 0 eludes interpretation — from table 2a or + from table 2b; the biphone is interpreted neither as non-monophonized nor as monophonized, but as non-existent, i.e., in the system there has arisen an empty position. The symmetrically situated boundary position in agreement with it has likewise been vacated, and in such a way that the dominant supporting monophonization is replaced by the subdominant, i.e., *t, d* > *k, g*. In the system a second position is thus symmetrically freed and a binary 0 appears:

	k, g	*p, b*	*t, d*
l	—	—	0
n	—	+	+
m	0	+	+

TABLE 2c

This compromise formation can have on the territory on which it develops, a quite different meaning. On conservative West Slavic territory this process means innovation. On the rest of the territory it means conservatism.

4.6 The following can be suggested for expressing the different periods for the change of the biphones *tl, dl* in a single formula: in Table 2' we designate the individual rows and columns according to a sequence of simple whole numbers:

χ ψ	1	2	3
1	1,1	2,1	3,1
2	1,2	2,2	3,2
3	1,3	2,3	3,3

TABLE 2'

Then the following results for N and 0 are valid:

For 2a: N for every $\chi / \psi / (\chi // \psi) = 1$ (primary rule)

For 2b: N for every $\chi + \psi < 4$

For 2c: 0 for $\chi - \psi = |2|$ (definition of boundary position).

5. RESULTS

(1) Proof and explanation of the meaning of the existence of change (1.3'). A lack of change, i.e. (1.1) may be structurally equivalent to change. For a difference in structure in the results, including the result N, no difference in structure is necessary.

(2) In the whole complex of changes of biphones formulated under 2.3, it is primarily in the biphones *tl, dl* that no changes occur. We are dealing, therefore, with a stable isogloss.

(3) Further processes, i.e., disintegration according to tables 2a, 2b, 2c, are more recent; they arise only as a result of this complex of changes. The different character does not rest on a difference of structures, which would indicate a real disintegration of unity, but on the different treatment of identical, but ambigious, elements of a unified strucure. The difference here is not, that is to say, caused by the underlying structure itself, but by the material (superficial) absence of an element.

(4) In the complex of changes of biphones this change is not only chronologically, but also chiefly systemically, somewhat marginal, so that it has won for itself the right to its "popularity" in linguistic textbooks not at all by virtue of its importance, but by the fact that it strikingly reveals the boundaries within the Slavic continuum.

CHAPTER II

THE PROTO-LANGUAGE AND ITS DISINTEGRATION

1. STAGES OF PROTO-SLAVIC AND ITS EXTINCTION

1.0   The isogloss of the fall of the jers has usually been designated as the terminal boundary of Common Slavic development, e.g., Trubetzkoy 1922, 217-218, Horálek 1962, 126: "the last Common Slavic change", Pauliny 1963, 78. Komárek 1962, 47, classes contraction and the fall of the jers with Czech phenomena; however, he stresses the fact that the changes in the jers have general relevancy.

Bernštejn 1961, 50-51, voices sharp protest against Trubetzkoy's concept; Shevelov 1964, 607, later states that this period, i.e., the period of changes in the jers, is still Slavic, though by no means Common Slavic.

1.1   To a certain extent this is, of course, a problem of a terminological dispute based on the question of what to call the period between unity and non-unity, the period of breakup, of the disintegration of unity. As we attempted to point out in Chapter I, even breakup is a feature of unity, for that which has already definitely lost its uniform character is unable to break up, so that only the last common step toward breakup is the definite end of unity. If it were necessary to say "yes" or "no", then it would be possible from these positions to defend the idea of Trubetzkoy, even though there can be no disputing that disjunctive isoglosses extend to the close of unity. If, however, it is a question of the dichotomy, "unity : non-unity", then disintegration belongs without a doubt to unity, indeed, to the period of non-compact isoglosses.

1.2   With regard to the nature of isoglosses, as formulated in Chapter I, it is possible to establish the following three stages in the development of unity:

(1) The compact stage ("Proto-Slavic")
(2) The non-compact stage ("Common Slavic")
(3) The disjunctive stage

In accordance with 1.1, we shall, therefore, also investigate the second stage as a stage of unity.

1.3 In accordance with Chapter I and with 1.2, we shall consider as the limit of a stage its last characteristic feature, which for conciseness can be called the final feature. The characteristic features of the following stage which chronologically precede this last feature, arising, so to speak, in the womb of the preceding stage, can be called embryonic features.

2. ON THE PLACE OF CONTRACTION IN THE DEVELOPMENT OF UNITY

2.0 For the establishment of the character of contraction two facts must be established, namely, whether the well-known differences in contraction among the various Slavic languages are only quantitative or qualitative and whether contraction precedes or follows the fall of the jers.

2.1 Bernštejn 1961, 247, when discussing contraction makes no fundamental distinction among the Slavic languages. (His viewpoint will be pursued further in IV). The differences, he says, have a chronological character: contraction is the automatic outcome of the fall of intervocalic *i,* which occurred in West Slavic before the fall of the jers, in South Slavic after it, in East Slavic much later still; in Czech it occurred much earlier than in Slovak, in Serbo-Croatian earlier than in Bulgarian.

2.2 Horálek 1962, 144 ff., takes a compromise position, pointing out that "the so-called 'contraction'. . · had already begun in the prehistoric period" and further, on 145, "in some regions it remained very limited". To illustrate this great limitation examples are adduced from Russian. This would mean that the original, perhaps still compact, development broke up and became territorially independent.

2.3 Shevelov 1964, wholly supports an unequivocal position in favor of the disjunctivity of contraction, though he states that it develops "particularly in the Adro-Baltic expanse" (524); but he contravenes the above restriction by taking the development in the word *pojasъ* to be an entirely typical instance of contraction in the individual languages; thus with all succinctness he has not only, as it were, exactly expressed his opinion on the boundary between languages that realize contraction, i.e., West Slavic, and languages that do not realize contraction, i.e.,

East Slavic, Bulgarian, but he has also fixed the boundary within certain languages where there are in this sense dialect differences, c.f. Slovenian, Serbo-Croatian *pās/pojas*.

2.4 We know, however, as Bernštejn and Horálek after all emphatically point out in the passage cited, that no language remained beyond the reach of contraction; on the other hand, neither did any language exploit all the possibilities, and not only for morphological reasons, but also for phonological reasons; this fundamentally undermines the notion that contraction is the automatic outcome of the fall of intervocalic elements. But the Shevelovian concept of a sharp boundary between languages with contraction and those without it is also threatened by it. The following table 3 illustrates the situation as it appears in basic features in reality:

		Po	US	LS	Cz	Sk	Sn	Sc	Bu	R	U	CV
1	*dobrajego*	I	I	I	I	I	I	I	I	I	I	20
2	*dělaješь*	+	I	I	I	I	I	I	I	–	+	16
3	*dobroje*	I	I	I	I	I	I	I	–	–	I	16
4	*pojasъ*	I	I	I	I	I	+	+	–	–	–	12
5	*sъměješь*	I	I	–	I	I	+	I	–	–	–	11
6	*vějati*	+	I	I	I	I	–	–	–	–	–	9
7	*ženojǫ*	I	–	–	I	+	I	+	–	–	–	8
8	*mojego*	+	+	–	I	+	I	+	–	–	–	8
9	*stojati*	+	–	–	I	I	+	–	–	–	–	6
10	*lajati*	–	I	–	I	+	–	–	–	–	–	5
11	*moja*	+	–	–	+	+	+	–	–	–	–	4
12	*vojevoda*	–	–	–	+	–	+	–	–	–	–	2
13	*zajęcь*	–	–	–	–	–	–	+	–	–	–	1
14	*směješь sę*	–	–	–	–	–	–	–	–	–	–	0
	TV	14	15	10	20	17	13	11	4	2	5	X
	TV'	15	15	10	22	18	15	12	4	2	5	X

TABLE 3

Explanatory notes:

1. Macedonian is included under Bulgarian, Belorussian under Russian. Languages with limited information, such as Polabian, have not been considered here.

2. The words in column 2 contain two vowels separated by *j*.

3. I designates a language having only contracted forms: two points.

+ designates a language having a contracted and an uncontracted form: one point.

— designates a language having only an uncontracted form: no points.

4. CV designates the contraction value, which determines the frequency of contraction in individual words.

TV designates the trend value, which determines the frequency of contraction in the individual languages (in the first 10 rows).

TV' designates an additional trend value that determines the frequency of contraction in an entire column.

3. COALESCENCE AND CONTRACTION, CONTRACTION LANGUAGES

3.0 This table does not pretend to comprehend all questions of contraction; however, since the most characteristic cases have been chosen as demonstrated by CV, the table fairly accurately elucidates the basic outlines of contraction.

3.1 On the vertical level, which expresses the differences in the realization of contraction in the various languages, it is possible to distinguish clearly two groups:

Group A (Polish — Serbo-Croatian), where TV $\geq$ 10

Group B (Bulgarian — Ukrainian), where TV $<$ 5

3.2.0 On the horizontal level, which expresses differences in the realization of contraction in individual cases, the first row, where CV reaches maximum, has been isolated. This row represents only certain clearly delineated cases.

3.2.1 The maximum in the type *dobrajego* is reached because even East Slavic, at first glance so conservative in contraction, shows here a change to *dobrogo*. But in a change of this type not phonetic impulses, but morphological ones, have a part, cf. Borkovskij and Kuznecov 1963, 244. There, to be sure, the intervention of phonetic factors is also admitted, but formulating it as contraction is expressly avoided. Similarly, historical grammars of the remaining East Slavic languages also shun this formulation, cf. Bezpalko et al. 1957, 275 ff., *Narysy pa historyji belaruskaj movy,* Minsk 1957, 169. The fact that, in contrast to the imperfect, the term "contraction", or "coalescence" (*stjaženie* etc.) does not appear in this case, indicates that the authors were avoiding this clear-cut formulation, and did so entirely deliberately. Horálek 1962, 144 ff., sees in the first stage, *dobraago,* the outcome of vocalic assimilation, in the second stage, *dobrago,* contraction. However, of the Russian forms *pustogo, pustomu,* he says that "they did not arise by contraction, but are forms formed directly (to be sure, our note) after the pronouns," 145. Bernštejn 1961, 247, cites forms of this type as the only examples of contraction in East Slavic. According to his hypothesis, the cases contracted most easily when both coalescing vowels were the same. One may ask both authors why, then, contraction did not occur by preference in such East Slavic forms as *sinii, sinjaja, sinee, sinče, sinjuju·* Because direct cases are involved. Morphological motivation within this process is here beyond any doubt. This isolated process, then, does not directly involve contraction.

3.2.2 Counter to this, changes in the imperfect may be understood as changes with phonetic motives and, therefore, as contraction. Is it, therefore, on the basis of this change, which also approximates the maximum CV, necessary to understand contraction as a Common Slavic process in which the individual languages or, if you will, language areas differ among themselves only in intensity of development? Horálek 1962, 145, regards this change as one type of contraction. However, as he himself acknowledges, this case differs from the remainder in that the two contracted vowels are not separated by an intervocalic *j* or, if you will, *i.* Krajčovič 1962, 111, fn. 1, expressly abandons this approach and regards as contraction only those cases with this intervocalic element. That contraction in the imperfect is not directly connected with the further process of contraction (i.e., as an impulse) has three arguments in its favor: this coalescence did not of itself lead to contraction, to which the languages of group B testify. The results of coalescence in the imperfect do not correspond to the results of coalescence in other cases. In the imperfect *ěa* $>$ *ě*, cf. *veděachъ*$>$ Old Polish *wiedziech,* Klemensiewicz et al. 1964, 367, *pletěachъ* $>$ Lower Sorbian *plešech,* Mucke 1891, 518, whereas in contraction *ěja* $>$ *a,* cf. Polish *siać,* Lower Sorbian *saś,* etc., Shevelov 1964, 526. Finally, it may be noted that coalescence in the imperfect gave, it is true, length, as was the case with contraction, but only the process of contraction established this length as a phonological category, i.e., length from coalescence survives only in the languages in which contraction is realized, cf. XIV/3.

3.2.3 The above-mentioned particulars quite clearly demonstrate that between coalescence in the imperfect and the entire complex of contraction there is only a loose relationship that can be formulated in these terms:

(1) Coalescence in the imperfect is the older phenomenon and did not provide a direct impetus for contraction.

(2) However, as soon as the impetus for contraction was given from other sources, the coalescence in the imperfect, more exactly, the already coalesced forms in the imperfect, come into contact with this process, cf. VII/3.4.

In connection with this we would like to call attention to two types of models that function entirely differently in language. In the case of coalescence, it is a question of a static model, i.e., a model that, indeed, can influence the form of similar formations, but cannot itself be the active force for change into this new form. The dynamic model, on the other hand, applies both these features; it determines the form but also serves as an impetus for the change.

3.2.4 Henceforth we shall construe as contraction only those cases with intervocalic *j,* cf. Krajčovič 1962, 111.

3.3 Rows 2-10 in table 3 represent the most frequent cases of contraction that entirely characteristically separate the languages of group A, in which, in principle, contraction is realized, and the languages of group B, in which contraction, in principle, does not occur: On cases of contraction in the group B ("transperipheral" languages) see the following chapter.

We shall, therefore, be calling the languages of group A "contraction languages" and the territory of these languages "contraction territory" and the languages of group B "non-contraction languages"; at the same time, it will not be a question of quantitative differences in the realization of contraction, but of the basic difference between presence and absence of contraction in the system. Thus a further question is also answered, to wit, whether the process of contraction is Protoslavic or not. The process of contraction encroached upon only a part of Slavic territory and is, therefore, a disjunctive change.

3.4 Rows 11-14 represent marginal cases. The cases were realized only over a very limited territory, and even here inconsistently, and represent one of the specifics of the individual Slavic (contraction) languages. In several cases, as in row 13, it is not even certain whether the change chronologically belongs to the process of contraction.

3.5 Row 14 represents numerous cases in which contraction was not realized for certain reasons and which exclude the thesis of contraction as an automatic outcome of the fall of intervocalic *j*.

4. SUMMARY

In summary of this chapter one may say that:

1. The concept in Shevelov 1964 of the disjunctivity of the process of contraction comprehends its essence. Also, the division into languages of the type *pas : pojas,* i.e., into contraction languages and non-contraction languages, must be regarded as successful.

2. The conception of contraction as a Common Slavic process is founded on a misunderstanding. Not every coalescence in the Slavic languages belongs to the process of contraction being investigated. The Common Slavic phenomenon of coalescence in the imperfect is not directly connected with the whole process, for it is realized also in languages that do not know contraction proper. Coalescence of the type *dobrojego > dobrogo,* if this is a matter of contraction at all, is not motivated phonetically, and phonetic character is the starting point for contraction. Coalescence in the imperfect is connected with contraction only secondarily. Another serious source of misunderstanding is the concept of the non-existence of a sharp boundary between contraction languages and non-contraction

languages. We have attempted to weaken this concept in table 3, which not only shows that the boundaries exist, but also that they are sufficiently clear cut, that not only quantitative differences between the languages, but also fundamental qualitative differences, can be determined. The fact that one may proceed thus not only between languages, but also within individual languages between dialects, also removes the last great barrier, namely, that the boundaries were always where the boundaries of languages formed later appear. This only attests to the ancient character of this process.

3. By this method the Slavic territory has been divided into contraction languages and dialects and non-contraction languages and dialects; thus, it has been established that the process of contraction is a disjunctive change.

4. This is not the place to discuss the question of the chronology of contraction, the concrete question of priority and succession between contraction and the fall of the jers, concerning which see XVII/2. It is generally accepted, though not completely proved, that contraction is a process that precedes the fall of the jers. If this hypothesis is true, then contraction is an embryonic symptom of the disjunctive stage.

CHAPTER III

CONTRACTION TERRITORY AND ITS DIVISION: FOCUS, CENTRAL AREA, PERIPHERY AND TRANSPERIPHERY

1. CONTRACTION TERRITORY, DIVISIONS WITHIN IT

The contraction territory and its boundaries were defined in II/3. However, neither within these boundaries, nor on the boundaries, nor even beyond the boundaries of this territory is the development entirely uniform, the TV's of the individual languages and dialects differ among themselves from one another. It is the task of this chapter to establish, with the help of the TV's, the territorial development of contraction.

We shall apply to this investigation the method by which in the preceding chapter we established the boundary between contraction languages and non-contraction languages, i.e., we shall take the TV of the relevant languages as the criterion of intensity of development, as we have shown. We shall proceed at the time from the familiar methodological postulate that languages situated nearer the focus of a process have undergone more intensive development, that languages on the peripheries reflect the process to a weaker degree (cf. wave theory). Intensity of development can be measured in the terms of the TV, that is, the higher the TV of a language, the closer it stands to the focus of the process of contraction.

2. THE FOCUS

2.0 Following table 3, it is not difficult to state that that Czech has the highest, i.e., the maximum, TV and hence is the focus of the contraction process.

2.1 Within a territory it is not a mater of mere quantitative difference, as though, that is to say, Czech simply had more cases than other languages; the maximum represents a new qualitative stage. This attribute is not due to accident or perhaps even to arbitrariness of choice in table 3, but it is a case of objective reality. That is to say, Czech contains the maximum of cases not only in the sense that it has more cases than any other, but also more than all the other languages combined, i.e., that — perhaps beyond isolated, patently secondary phenomena of the type Serbo-Croatian *zec* — in general, there is no case in another language that would be unknown to Czech. Thus in Czech as the focus of contraction this process reached its maximum extent.

2.2 The special position of Czech among the other Slavic languages was observed long ago. Thus Gebauer (1893, repr.) 1963, says of contraction: "But there is nevertheless an obvious quantitative difference in this matter: in Czech, short forms are more frequent . . . ". Shevelov 1964, 527, rightly concludes from this feature of Czech that "the center of the contractions lay in Cz" (i.e., Czech).

2.3 It is, of course, not so important by what means the inference concerning the key position of Czech was reached. However, it is important that the proper conclusions were not drawn from this, i.e., the necessity to investigate conclusively the system of Slavic contraction from the position of the focus, from the position of structure to the maximum extent of this process. But as Komárek — nearly 70 years after Gebauer — confirms in his *Gebauerovo historické hláskosloví ve světle dalšího bádání* (Gebauer's historical phonology in the light of further research in appendix to Gebauer 1963), 730, with the words, "the shape of coalescence, as Gebauer gives it . . . , has changed only in particular details", no systematic research into the substance has been implemented in this structure. Systematic investigation of Czech contraction is, therefore, the starting point for the investigation of this territorially very broad process.

3. THE CENTRAL REGION

To this region belong, in addition to the focus, those languages that in intensity of development most closely approach the focus.

3.1 Judging by TV, here in the first place belong Slovak and Upper Sorbian.

3.2 In the case of Slovak, however, a cautious approach is necessary. If we analyze the individual dialects, then we find that in Slovak territory there are regions where the TV also approaches maximum (in the western region, for example), so that, accurately stated, the focus extends beyond the later boundary of the Czech language, which need not at all be without connection with the political siutation (the era of Great Moravia comes readily to mind). On the other hand, the Central Slovak region shows a TV of 14 and thus wrenches itself — though partially and for other reasons — to a certain extent from the central region and falls together with some dialects of South Slavic. On the other hand, contemporary East Slovak dialects would obviously belong to the central region.

3.3 Other languages dialectally differentiated also require similarly cautious treatment. Thus, the Polish TV of 14 actually conceals two very different values. The South Polish dialects have in reality a TV of 17, thus surpassing Upper Sorbian, whereas the North Polish dialects show a TV of 8, which assigns them a place on the farthest edge of contraction territory. Similarly, in Slovenian there are dialects with a TV of 16 which without doubt belong to the central region, while in other dialects the TV may likewise fall below 10.

3.4 After a more detailed investigation of TV in the individual languages, we shall find that the West Slovak territory also belonged to the focus area, and that the forerunners of Upper Sorbian, South Polish, East Slovak, and North Slovenian belonged to the central region beyond the focus. These dialects in the period of contraction immediately adjoined the focus. The other dialects are situated beyond this region.

3.5 A more detailed investigation of the dialects could lead to still more accurate results. But even now it is clear that it is precisely the investigation of contraction which can fix the exact territorial connections among the Proto-Slavic dialects even prior to the formation of the historical languages: connections such as that of Czech with Slovenian and the deep penetration of Central Slovak into the South Slavic continuum. Furthermore, the elements of contraction in the dialect of Dubrovnik, cf. Belić 1962, 1, 128, supposes a Čakavian substratum.

28

4. THE PERIPHERY

4.1 To the periphery belong those contraction languages, or dialects, that do not belong to the central region. This concerns those systems whose TV is close to 10 or, as pointed out in III/3, slightly below 10.

4.2 TV in Serbo-Croatian is also worthy of investigation. In Čakavian it reaches a value of 14, which approaches that of the central region. Elsewhere, however, it may fall below 10.

4.3 Here it must be asked whether it is necessary to reformulate the definition of contraction languages as languages with a TV $>$ 10, for dialects with 10 $>$ TV $>$ 4 would not belong to a single group of languages. A new formulation would be in place if it were possible to fix the boundary of the periphery, particularly in South Slavic territory, between contraction dialects and non-contraction dialects. That it would be possible to determine this boundary after more detailed investigation is not entirely excluded, however it is more likely a question of there having been a transitional zone here to which only a few features of contraction penetrated. We might most likely also explain some phenomena in the transperiphery that way.

5. THE TRANSPERIPHERY

5.0 By transperiphery we mean that part of the non-contraction languages or dialects that were secondarily encroached upon by contraction isoglosses. They are, then, those systems that lie in close proximity to the periphery (where we also assign a transitional zone), that is, Bulgarian, with Macedonan, and Ukrainian.

5. Shevelov 1964, 527, says of Macedonian and Bulgarian: "M(acedonian) and B(ul)g(arian) had only a few morphologically conditioned contractions". It is not here a matter of cases of the type *dobrajego* $>$ *dobrogo,* known from the Old Bulgarian period, of course, cf. Mirčev 1963, 159, which we exluded from our considerations in II/3.2.1, but still chiefly a question of the rise of a new conjugation of the type *săbiram* (cf. op. cit., 188), which, as the author points out, is most extensive in the West Bulgarian dialects. He also cites the analogical integration of thematic and athematic verbs in most Slavic languages, by

which he evidently wants to show that it is a question of parallel
development. But the fundamental difference between Bulgarian
and Macedonian on the one hand and the other languages with
this type of contraction is that they are contraction languages
in which, therefore, this integration between thematic and
athematic verbs was realized as a result of the contraction of the
forms of the type *dělaješь* > *děláš*. Because it would be para-
doxical to seek in Bulgarian and Macedonian a completely different development with the same outcome, it is necessary to state
that the contracted forms penetrated as a morphological isogloss even across the boundary of the contraction territory. This
is attested by, among other things, the circumstances that the
Bulgarian dialects lying nearer to this territory undergo this
process much more intensively: the ending *-m* in he 1st person
sing. is generalized, which only confirms the morphological
character of the whole process. The first such endings in Bulgarian are attested from the 14th century (cf. Mirčev, loc. cit),
in Serbo-Croatian from the 13th century (cf. Belić 1962, 2, 57),
where there are, of course, contracted forms as a result of a
prehistoric process of contraction (ibid., 54). Is it true though,
that contraction as a motivated phonetic process was realized in
the whole Serbo-Croatian territory or some eastern dialects of
Serbo-Croatian territory were here and perhaps also elsewhere
the predecessors of Bulgarian and Macedonian in the transperipheral process?

5.2. Mirčev, when he was speaking of languages that have
realized the integration of thematic and athematic verbs, patently
did not have in mind non-contraction Ukrainian. It, of course,
likewise belongs to the transperiphery, even though analogical
morphological incursions of contracted forms were obviously
realized rather earlier, obviously not so smoothly, perhaps not
so profoundly, but clearly on a large scale. It is not unwarranted
to relate these changes to the context of the political conditions.

5.2.1 It is self-evident that even here dialects lying in
direct proximity with West Slavic languages, i.e., with contraction
territory, are subject most to the influence. But where forms like
znam, znaš are adopted along with forms of the type *znawem,
znalam*, it may be difficult to speak of a connection with the
contraction process. On the other hand, the Carpathian forms
of the 3rd person sing., *znat', dumat'*, are indeed an application

of contraction to the morphological system, not a simple adoption of the West Slavic form without final *t'*; in such a system it is indeed possible to speak of "morphological contraction", parallel with Bulgarian contraction.

5.2.2 Unfortunately, Bezpalko et al. 1957, who in the case of the Carpathian forms of the 2nd person sing. (citing *znaš, dumaš*) speak of a lost affix of the root (p. 327), and in the 1st person — examples *spivam, dumam* — consider only of the influence of athematic verbs (p. 326), do not throw much light on this question. Here it is, of course, as in Bulgarian and Macedonian, a question of morphological contraction with consequences for the entire paradigm.

5.2.3 Of greater consequence, because it is also territorially more significant, is, of course, the problem of contraction in the compound declension of adjectives. The possibility that here it is a question of some kind of contamination between the nominal and the "compound" declensions does not enter into consideration, for the system of adjectives so changed bears all the earmarks of contraction; especially characteristic here are the contraction *oje* > *e* in the neuter and *yji* > *i* in the plural (where after contraction the hardness of the preceding consonant was retained). Bezpalko et al. 1957, 284 ff., have no answer to the question of the rise of these forms; however, they do cite a parallel with the pronominal declension and the Old Russian forms (cf. also the type *dobrogo*). But in both cases it is a question of phenomena extending to all of East Slavic, so that they are unable to tell us much about the specifics of Ukrainian. Furthermore, if it were a question of an old contraction, the long outcome in the neuter would have to be reflected as *i* in Ukrainian. On the other hand, Bezpalko et al. 1957, 282, offer the valuable finding that these coalesced forms penetrate as far as the 14th-15th centuries and that some dialects, including even the Carpathian (!, 286) do not have coalesced forms. Even though Bezpalko talks here of coalescence, this is not a phonetic phenomenon since in other cases, identically phonetically conditioned, coalescence was not realized. Rather it is above all a morphological process.

5.2.4 There is a definite reluctance to couple this Ukrainian process with the analogous process in the West Slavic languages. Of course, on purely linguistic grounds this skepticism is excessive. That is to say, it is not a question of the acceptance of complete morphological forms, which acceptance might indeed lead to a negative attitude. This phenomenon has, on the contrary, the features of an expanding isogloss — it is a question of two related, adjoining systems; one system affords an attractive, dynamic model for the appropriate developments in the other system, so that there is here no fundamental difference between Bulgarian and Ukrainian. The fact that the Carpathian dialect does not have coalesced forms shows that this isogloss expanded to Ukrainian via Polish, which is a further reason why it is simply a model that Ukrainian applied to its system, cf. the Polish accusative *dobrą*, the Ukrainian *dobruju* > *dobru;* the Polish instrumental *dobrą*, the Ukrainian without contraction.

5.2.5 Here and in table 3 we do not take into consideration cases of the type *mojoho* > *moho, mojeji* > *moji* (cf. Bezpalko et al. 1957, 258). We assume that adjoining contraction dialects did not realize contraction here. Are there, then, also indigenous morphological motivations for contraction?

5.3 Transperipheral phenomena, therefore, are connected with secondary morphological consequences of contraction that cross the boundary of contraction territory and as new isoglosses penetrate even into neighboring systemically close languages and dialects.

6. ON CONTRACTION IN NORTH RUSSIAN DIALECTS

6.1 In North Russian (NR) dialects, there is a process which reminds one of the contraction which occurs in West Slavic and West South Slavic dialects (cf. *pojas* > *pās*, Shevelov, 1964, 524). That is why Bernštejn 1968, 19ff. criticizes those who ignore the Russian facts and maintain that contraction is limited to West Slavic (more exactly including West South Slavic) dialects. However, contraction (universally) is one of the most common intersyllabic changes and it would be very doubtful to suppose that this fact has been ignored by Slavists up to now.

6.1 What is more important is the question of

(1) whether these processes, i.e. the NR change and contraction, can be identified territorially, chronologically, and typologically, which would have immense consequences both for

the conception of Proto-Slavic unity and for the history of Russian itself, or

(2) whether we face two completely different phenomena which seem similar only because they affect very closely related languages, but whose motivations are, rather, universal.

The following reasons exclude the first possibility:

a. *Territorial*: The territory of contraction does not affect Ukrainian changes like *dobraja* > *dobra* and especially West Ukrainian transperipheral changes which are of later date (see III/5). Also, South Russian contraction is very sporadic and no phenomena indicate that this process could be of any importance for these dialects. Thus, the isolation of the NR process from the contraction territory is obvious; there are no direct territorial connections between these two processes.

b. *Chronological*: There is no doubt that contraction is in immediate chronological contact with the jer shift (loss of jers). Already in 1894 it was conclusively proved that contraction had to precede the Czech change *a* > *ě*, which occured in the 12th or 13th century (Gebauer 1963, 555 ff). On the other hand, the NR change is still in process, see Bernštejn 1968, 21, and the coexistence of both contracted and non-contracted forms, such as *znaet/znaat/znat,* is usual in NR dialects. Consequently, there is also an important chronological differcence between the two processses.

c. *Typological*: The processes have completely different places in the structure:

ca. The NR process does not occur if the stress follows immediately after *j* cf. *dajot, stojál* etc. (Bernštejn 1968, 21), while there are no contraction cases in which the stress would be relevant for its development·

cb. The NR process does not have any essential phonological consequences for the system and the morphological consequences are very limited, c.f. the oppositions NR Fem. Nom. *ta* : *dobra,* i.e., with identification of the ending, analogous to the common Russian Masc. Gen. Dat. etc. *togo, tomu . . · : dobrogo . . .*; in comparison with Old Czech *ta* : *dobrá, tu* : *dobrú, toho, tomu . . . : dobrého, dobrému . . .*

cc. The NR process is limited to certain morphological categories, especially to certain forms of adjectives and verbs. In contraction there are no such limitations and the process affects all inflectional categories.

6.3   Conclusion: Even this brief examination is sufficient to indicate that the NR process has no direct relation to contraction. It can be compared with it only as a certain analogous model. Thus, its only use for comparison with contraction might be in reconstructing a sequence of the steps between the original group *aje* and the result *ā*, i.e., *aje* > *ae* > *aa* > *ā*, cf. NR forms in b. But even this is both highly hypothetical and, which is more important, actually irrelevant for contraction, if this is regarded and investigated as a deep structure phenomenon.

7.   Diagram of the areas of contraction:

The results of this chapter may be summarized in the following diagram (1):

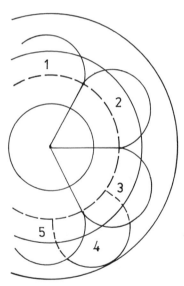

DIAGRAM 1

Key to the diagram:
   I.   The concentric circles represent the boundaries of the regions:
   1. inner circle — boundary of the focus (Czech with West Slovak)
   2. broken circle (- - -) — boundary of the central region
   3. the two complete circles delimit the "outer periphery" (i.e., the

transitional zone); the adjoining inner region represents the periphery proper, the adjoining outer region represents the transperiphery.

II. The lines radiating from the center and the semicircles attached to them represent the boundaries of the individual languages, as follows (reading clockwise): 1. Sorbian (inside the broken circle — Upper, outside — Lower), 2. Polish (inside — South, outside — North), 3. Slovak (inside — East, outside — Central), 4. Serbo-Croatian (inside — Čakavian, outside — Štokavian), 5. Slovenian (inside — North, outside — South).

PART TWO

STAGES OF CONTRACTION

CHAPTER IV

THE PRE-CONTRACTION PHONOLOGICAL SYSTEM
AND THE MOTIVATIONS FOR CONTRACTION

1. COALESCENCE AND CONTRACTION

1.0 Coalescence is usually understood as the fusing of the vowels of two adjacent syllables not separated by a consonant (or a group of consonants) into a single long vowel. It is sometimes said, of course, that the vowels are separated by an intervocalic element *j*, but in practice such cases are not distinguished from those in which this element is not present, cf. Komárek 1962, 45, (e.g., *nesĕachъ*), Shevelov 1964, 524 ff. (e.g., *bĕachъ* on 526).

1.1 The definition of coalescence in 1.0 can be expressed symbolically as

$$TA^1 \ \& \ A^2 \rightarrow TA, \qquad (4)$$

where

1) A is a vowel
2) T is a nonvowel
3) & is an intervocalic element which does not prevent contraction
4) 1, 2 are indices of the order of equal elements
5) A^1, A^2 are vowels separated by & (hereafter *contrahends*)
6) ¯(macron) is length resulting from contraction
7) A is a long vowel resulting from contraction, hereafter *contract*
8) A^1 & A^2 is a contracting cluster

1.2 These rules of relationships are binding for the expressions in 1.1:

1. Expressions except the procedent are synchronic facts.

2. The order of the individual members of the contracting cluster and the other elements in the formula, as well as the direction of the process, are given by this formula without exception.

3.   In respect to rule 2, it is possible to cite individual parts of this formula in relation to expressions of the same category (e.g., contrahends and contract in relation to other vowels).

1.3   The expression T was formulated as a non vowel. If the formula is to be universally valid, however, then it follows that in cases of the type *dobraja, stryjьcь, myslěaše,* etc., T represents any nonvowel, i.e., also a cluster of consonants.

1.4.0   From 1.1 it follows that as cases of the type *dobraja, dějachъ* underwent coalescence, so did cases of the type *volaachъ, děachъ.* In the first set of cases there is assumed between the contrahends the presence of that element that is written as *j, i* and that is reflected as the phoneme *j* in a projection to the historical stages of the Slavic languages. This phonological unit we shall write as I and its intervocalic variant we shall write as &i. In the second set of cases we shall assume the absence of that element and we shall write this correlate of the segments as 0 and &o. In the case of ø, therefore, it is not by any means a question of the absence of a phoneme, but of a positional absence in which the phoneme I may be present.

1.4.1   Because &i, &o are the only two intervocalic elements that do not prevent contraction, it holds good that

$$\& = \&i \, / \, \&o \qquad\qquad (4.1.4)$$

1.4.2   These elements have the following relationship:

	type	shape of &	variants of
1	*dobraja*	&i	I
2	*volaachъ*	&o	ø

TABLE 4

Because it holds true that the element I can stand only between vowels or in the word-initial position, it holds true also for ø. Because of the fact, that every segment standing before an A is a T, it holds true also for I and ø, so that I//ø = T. However, because I, ø are not a cluster of consonants, and neither of them can enter into such clusters, they are, therefore, neither a consonant nor cluster of consonants and therefore, are nonvowel nonconsonats symbolised by M. Because the remaining primary nonvowels can form clusters, I, ø are the only nonvowel nonconsonants. It holds true, therefore, that

$$M = I/ø \qquad (4.1)$$

1.5 According to II/3.2, by contraction we understand only the cases

$$TA\&iA \rightarrow TA \qquad (4')$$

or following table 4

$$TAIA \rightarrow TA \qquad (4!)$$

These cases will be the subject of investigation in subsequent chapters. The problem of the phonetic motivation of contraction is related to the question of the development of the element &i, i.e., of intervocalic *j*.

2. CONTEMPORARY CONCEPTS OF THE DEVELOPMENT OF INTERVOCALIC *j* (&i).

2.0 Contemporary concepts assume that the initial motivation for contraction is the intervocalic development

$$I \rightarrow ø \qquad (4.2)$$

that is,

$$\&i \rightarrow \&o \qquad (4.2')$$

cf. e.g., the formulation in Komárek 1962, 445: "By coalescence we understand the merging of two vowels which were separated from each other by intervocalic *j* (*i*) into a single vowel. The basis for merging is the loss of intervocalic *j*." Similarly, for example, Shevelov 1964, 524. We find an elucidation of this concept in Krajčovič 1962 and Bernštejn 1961.

2.1 Krajčovič pictures process (2) as occurring in stages, i.e., so that the development

$$TA_1\&iA_2 \rightarrow TA_1\&oA_2 \qquad (4.2.1)$$

is valid originally only for such cases wherein the contrahends were phonetically close to &i, i.e. $A^1/A^2 \cong$ &i (the cluster tьie is cited), from which arose the unstable state

$$TA^1\&o/\&iA^2 \tag{4.2.1'}$$

which was eliminated by the general process $(4.2.1)^1$.

2.2   In Bernštejn's concept, the process (4,2) is the outcome of the development $j > i > \emptyset$. Similarly, like Krajčovič, he points out that i was not a vowel, that therefore it did not coincide with the general structure of the syllable and that therefore it easily underwent changes. Contrary to Krajčovič, he is of the opinion that development (4.2') occurred in all positions simultaneously; only the merging of the contrahends into the contract is itself accelerated; if the phonological relationship $A^1 = A^2$ is valid, development beyond that toward this state, i.e., $A^1 \mid A^2 \rightarrow A^1 = A^2$, is assumed in the remaining cases.

2.3   The basic difficulty with concept (4.2'), whether in Krajčovič's stage concept or in Bernštejn's direct form, is the indisputable fact that this process does not have any kind of universal validity, that in a number of cases segment I was not eliminated. If this development actually was universally valid — and the authors do not set any limit to it — then, in such attested forms as *kraj, stoju, kupuješ*, the element I would again have to arise, i.e., the process $I \rightarrow \emptyset \rightarrow I$ would occur. This the authors rightly reject, for already the first stage would have, as a result, according to their concept, the deformation of the contracting cluster, resulting in the merging of the contrahends into the contract. But how was the process $I \rightarrow \emptyset$ regulated to avoid this contradiction? It is obvious that it is precisely the contrahends which played a more active role in this process.

3.   THE RISE OF PRIMARY CONTRACTION

3.1   Thus it is possible to turn to Krajčovič's previously cited thesis on the decisive influence of such clusters wherein

---

1) Author's formulation: ". . . in cases of the type **tьie** for phonetic reasons non-syllabic **i** merged with adjacent related elements, with the result that it lost any **phonetic** (emphasis added) validity and disappeared even in cases of the type **tоie**." Did not the author have in mind **phonological** validity, i.e., that the absence of **i** meant the same as its **presence**?

A1//A2 $=$ I. It is obvious that *i, ь* are such contrahends; the distinction *i* : *ь* is only a matter of quantitative correlation, which is irrelevant for the process of contraction, as, e.g., *pěší* $\langle$ *pěšiji*// *pěšьjь* indicate. Likewise irrelevant for contraction is the relationship *i* : *y, ь* : *ъ,* for the quality of the contract does not depend on the relationship of the individual contrahends, but on the presence or absence of softness in the preceding T. This rule of the influence of T on the phonetic (and not the phonological!) modification of the contrahend, then, is quite wrongly supplanted by the notion that A1 is crucial for the quality of the contract, cf. Krajčovič 1962, 114.

3.2 It is possible, therefore, for the investigation of contraction, to group contractions of the sounds *i, ь, y, ъ* under one generic symbol ı, i.e., ı $= i/ь/y/ъ$. It is obvious that of all possible contrahends this ı is phonetically closest to the sound I, as the distinction ı : I is positional, i.e. allophonic only Process (4!) fully applies if A1//A2 $=$ ı, i.e., if it has the form

$$\text{TıIı} \rightarrow \text{Tı̄} \tag{4.3}$$

3.3 The generality and obligatoriness of this process is not trivial. Process (4.3), in contrast to other processes (4!) — aside from cases in XI which are obviously later — is valid in the face of *all* morphological barriers. That is why the imperative contracts, e.g. *kryji, šiji, pьji* $>$ *krý, ší, pí,* though all other imperatives of thematic verbs assume an ending -*i* and at the same time the preservation of the present stem, c.f. *laji, prěji, čuji; kryješь . . . ; laješь . . . ;* similarly, contracted *stryjьcь* $>$ *strýcь* is opposed to uncontracted *ujьcь,* the contracted substantive nom. *kyjь* $>$ *ký,* but gen. *kyja* is opposed to *krajь, kraja . . . staja,* etc. (*prijьdešь* $>$) *prídešь,* (*vyjьdešь* $>$) *výdešь* against *na-jьdešь* and *pri-nesešь, vy-nesešь* and a number of others .

3.4 Contraction (4.3) we shall call PRIMARY or phonetic CONTRACTION. On its character and consequences for the system see subsequent chapters, particularly IV.

4. SYLLABIC HARMONY AND &·

4.0 Prior to contraction there held true the general rule according to which "the whole syllable was either soft or hard", that is, both the frontness of a vowel and the softness of the preceding T was either present or absent. From the standpoint of these features it is possible to express the syllable thus:

$$T'A/T^-A \qquad (4.4)$$

where the symbol (') expresses the presence of both features and the symbol ($^-$) the absence of both features and T a consonant or M. If we write (')/($^-$) as (+), expression (4.4) can be written as

$$(TA)^+ \qquad (4.4')$$

which expresses the rule of concurrent presence or absence of a front vowel and softness of a preceding primary non-vowel or the law of SYLLABIC HARMONY.

Because presence : absence of a particular feature is qualified as the proportion markedness : unmarkedness, it is sometimes possible to omit the special symbol for the unmarked member. Thus, for example, the correlation T : T ' can also be written as t : t. '. This notation then shows that the marked correlate t' contains all the features of t and, moreover, the feature of frontness as well. We shall omit this formulation not only for its imprecision — that is, if t ' has the feature frontness, it does not have at the same time the feature backness — but also because the expression of T would be substantially complicated by it.

4.1 Now we shall designate
1) X as T/A
2) Y as the other segment in the sequence TA
3) X' as T'/'A
4) (XY)' as T'A, i.e. T' as well as 'A

The formulae (4.4) = (4.4') can be then expressed as

$$(XY)'/(XY)^- = (XY)^+ \qquad (4.4a)$$

If only one member of the sequence XY is marked the following rule applies:

$$X'Y \rightarrow (XY)' \qquad (4.4!)$$

that is, from the markedness of one member follows the same feature of the whole sequence and consequently also the markedness of both members. This feature, formulated in (4.4!), is termed the *marked harmonization of the syllable*. During the rise of contraction this process is already in essence complete, so that in the area of the most intensive contraction, i.e., in the central region, this process, together with principle (4.4) and (4.4!), from which it began, is suppressed. On the periphery these principles still offer considerable resistance.

4.2 In a syllable IA it is necessarily true that the vowel has the form 'A; in a syllable øA, on the other hand, it is necessarily true that the vowel has the form ⁻A. That means that I is the kind of M after which 'A follows, so that according to (4.4)

$$IA = M'A \tag{4.4.2a}$$

$$øA = M^-A \tag{4.4.2b}$$

and consequently

$$I = M' \tag{4.4.2a'}$$

$$ø = M^- \tag{4.4.2b'}$$

which is an application of the law of syllabic harmony to T = M.

Because &i, &o are variants of I, ø, it is valid for them that

$$\&i = \&' \tag{4.4.2a''}$$

$$\&o = \&^- \tag{4.4.2b''}$$

4.3 Because in the pair M', M⁻ only the contrast softness vs. hardness is of interest, it would be possible to formulate I as ø', and, therefore, &i as &'o, so that it would be valid that

$$IA = ø'A \tag{4.4.3}$$

This relationship is usually formulated as a redundancy, a "phonological pleonasm", cf. Mareš 1956, 471, of the sound *j*. But this formulation assumes that the correlation ⁻A : 'A is necessarily phonological, i.e., that no 'A is merely a variant of ⁻A, which is not valid, e.g. for *u, o* and, as a matter of fact, also for *y*. The redundancy of *j*, i.e., its phonological absence, would elevate the status of cases of the type *ju, jo*, etc., to that of new phonemes. It is obvious that from such a formulation one cannot expect accuracy. Therefore, it is more pertinent to hold to formulae (4.4.2a-2a'), which may be expressed in words as follows: the elements I : ø, i.e., M' : M⁻ differ only in one distinctive feature.

4.4 This shows that *j*, i.e., I, M', was not only phonetically realized but also had its own phonological validity, which, *inter alia*, explains why the loss of &i did not occur automatically, but according to certain rules, outside of which it survived as a phoneme. It still remains to explain the variability between the possibility of loss and further existence, for which the "surface" definition of contraction as a phonetic change is far from sufficient.

4.5 In IV/1.4.0 the element ø was defined as the absence of the element I, i.e., of the phoneme *j*. By this the element ø was brought into correlation with I; in view of this correlation we have avoided the desriptive, and consequently to a certain extent misleading, term "zero"; nevertheless, ø has a function analogous to that which, for example, the zero morpheme has, cf., e.g., the correlation M ' : M⁻ which fully corresponds to the regular opposition T' : T⁻. That is why ø = M⁻ is to be dèfined a PHONEME so that the synchronic shape of (prehistoric) syllable

$$(TA)^+ \tag{4.5}$$

(for T — consonant, consonantal cluster or M) is generally valid.

This notion, of course, interferes with "linguistic intuition". These and further interferences are not, to be sure, meaningless, because they do not rest on a negation of reality, but on its different formulation. Our "intuition" at the same time is opposed not to a concept of the contents themselves, which is not so different, but to the different relationship of the surface forms to their underlying contents. A zero element can deform a form; if the content survives, the relationship changes: in the word *zub* (Russian, Czech) there is a zero ending; the phonetician investigating this form states that the final consonant is realized as *p*. The surface form, a phenomenon, here does not correspond to the content, to the structural relationships. ø deforms similarly. It makes impossible the coexistence of two syllables separated by it; and this, by the way, without regard to the later fortunes of contraction, i.e., on the entire Slavic territory. And despite this primary independence of contraction and its Common Slavic nature, this deformation has an entirely different position in contracting and non-contracting systems.

4.6 Because, according to 4.2 and 4.3, I differs from the phoneme ø only by one distinctive feature, the same fate from the point of view of surface investigation is supposed. In reality, however, this distinctive feature is used by the system in an entirely different manner. Even the non-contraction languages, which used this systemic situation only for concrete morphological needs (coalescence of the type *dobrajego*) without any other systemic, i.e., phonological, consequences, clearly show this. The phoneme I differs from ø in one feature: it is not necessary for it, in order that contraction may occur, to disappear in advance; it can preserve its existence everywhere where the contrahends are not, for given reasons, able to contract. This ability or inability and its realization belong to the following chapters of contraction.

CHAPTER V

INTRODUCTION TO THE PHASIC TYPOLOGY OF CONTRACTION

1. CONTRACTION AS A COMPLEX PROCESS

1.0   We designate contraction as a multilateral process because it manifests factors stemming from various levels of language.

1.1.0   Empirically contraction is, as indeed every coalescence — cf. IV/1 ff. — a phonetic process. It is therefore evident that even PRIMARY FACTORS, i.e., factors that introduce the process of contraction into the system and thus mediate it for the system, MUST BE PHONETIC.

1.1.1   This primariness, as was shown in the preceding chapter, sometimes leads to its confusion with generality, to the interpretation of the whole process as a mechanical one bound to the single phonetic condition I $\rightarrow$ ø, leading to such paradoxes as the necessary consequence I $\rightarrow$ ø $\rightarrow$ I, cf. IV/2.

1.1.2   Authors who treat contraction as a whole, i.e., who consider cases of contraction in the aggregate, but simultaneously even cases with unrealized contraction, must relinquish this paradox and examine also systemic factors of development as well.

1.1.3   Negative systemic factors, i.e., factors impeding contraction, are stressed in, e.g., Komárek 1962, 46, where even the rise of doublets is explained this way. Shevelov 1964, 526 ff, proceeds similarly; however, he regards certain cases without contraction — e.g., Cz. *krájati* not as non-realization, as does Komárek 1962, but as restitution.

1.1.4   The most important hypothesis concerning systemic influences in Shevelov 1964 is the treatment by positive systemic factors not only of cases where phonetic influence is excluded, but also of cases where it is not proved. The author finds exclusively systemic impulses in such cases as *iji* $>$ *í, ǫjǫ* $>$ *ǫ́, ěja* $>$ *á,* etc. In Bulgarian and Macedonian phonetic factors are, in general, excluded.

1·2.0 The authors cited formulate systemic factors as MORPHOLOGICAL reasons. That means, in essence, that the authors regard as a development of contraction the opposition phonetic development: morphological development.

1.2.1 The underlying system does not participate in the spontaneous phonetic development; only superficial changes, i.e., changes in form, are here realized. They are realized with total disregard for the system, indeed even counter-systemically, and this not only on the morphological plane (liquidation of the boundaries of morphemes, but also of entire morphemes, typologically from agglutinative and analytic formations to synthetic formations) but equally so on the phonological plane (the rise of the contract with quantity not bound to the established prosodic system). Thus far, the viewpoint is quite objectively superficial. Of course, a new form may hide in itself an old content; a primary deformation need not yet affect the underlying structure.

1.2.2 The underlying process is characterized by the fact that it applies its own systemic considerations and interests to contraction. Thus, for example, the change $aja > á$ does not occur without exception, but only under favorable conditions, because it is a systemic change. The fact that even the underlying system is connected to the process shows that the process of contraction affected, at this stage, not merely superficial form, but also the underlying system itself that the surface mediated change in the underlying system, that, therefore, it is a question of deformation of another degree.

1.3.0 However, not even a systemic process is uniform i.e., equally "deep". It does not hold true without exception that the phonological and the morphological system must apply the same considerations; it is not even valid for subsystems within these systems.

1.3.1 In a systemic process, therefore, we determine the individual stages according to which factors predominate. In the case $A^1 = A^2$ — with the exception of cases with I in (4.3), cf. IV/3 — (4!) is always valid, except in morphologically motivated cases. It is necessary to treat differences in contraction territory among cases of the type *láti : lajati* thus: that on the periphery this stage conceivably manifested itself with less intensity, so that morphological factors offered greater resistance.

The lack of phonological barriers is to be interpreted by the fact that this stage was realized according to phonological rules.

1.3.2 In a further stage, wherein the formal condition for contraction is the only close proximity of both contrahends, i.e., $A1 = A2$, there survive certain phonological motives. In a case of the type *pojasъ* $>$ *pásъ*, which was a criterion for the contraction of a language, cf. II/2, there were no morphological grounds for contraction. Likewise, in the case *dobrějemь* $>$ *dobrěmь* morphological motivation is excluded. On the other hand, certain obviously morphological motivations do assert themselves. Where the contraction *lajati* $>$ *láti* is realized, the contraction *sějati* $>$ *šáti* is now realized in parallel manner. It is necessary to seek morphological motivation also in a change of the type *uměješь* $>$ *uměšь*, cf. *prosišь*, *dobroje* $>$ *dobré*, cf. *dobrá*, *dobrý*, *pěšě*, *moja* $>$ *má*, cf. *dobrá*, etc. Territorial modifications are determined by the distance of a language from the focus: the closer to the focus, the more changes. This gives evidence of the presence of morphological factors. But the contraction *vojevoda* $>$ *vévoda*, which is realized only at the focus and in the closest dialects, shows that at the focus even more phonological factors assert themselves in contraction.

1.3.3 A further phase, in which the only phonological condition is the formal condition of a certain degree of proximity of both contrahends, i.e. $A1 \sim A2$, transfers the stimulus for the realization of contraction entirely to morphological factors.

1.3.4 In the concluding stage of systemic contraction, which has to complete the morphological consequences of previous contractions, there is no place at all for formal and phonological conditions; the relationship of the contrahends is here irrelevant; in turn the greater are the claims laid on morphological motives·

1.3.5 In the final stage of the whole process, when the possibilities of direct systemic influence have been exhausted, there occurs a new spontaneous stage when the single condition for the realization of contraction is $A1 = ь(ъ)$. This stage, of course, produces new morphological types in the area of the substantive, whereby it fills the gap which existed in the morphological category of contract. Through this, in a certain general sense, the intention of the morphological system is realized. But these intentions — in contradistinction to preceding phases — can have destructive consequences as well. If they were invoked — and their universal character in all the contraction languages points to that — then, like the sorcerer's apprentice, they are not able to prevent its consequences, which in total disregard of morphology, destroy such relationships as *kryješь, šiješь* : *pь ješь pěšь; staja, šija* : *zmьja* > *zm'á*, etc.

2. SURVEY OF THE STAGES OF CONTRACTION

2.0   The development described in 1.3 has its own organic explanation both on the surface and in the underlying system.

2.1   On the surface we find a reduction in claims on the relationships of contrahends. The initially strict requirement that contrahends must be mutually identical to and simultaneously similar to I, is at a further stage limited only to mutual identity, then to close approximation, mere approximation and then to the irrelevance of the relationships of the contrahends until the strict formal condition $A^1 = b$ again recurs.

2.2   In the underlying system there is to be observed an interplay among the various planes and within them. On the first level (phonetics) there are in general no systemic rules. At the next stage, when form mediates changes in content, when phonetic form achieves harmony with the phonological system, when the rules for phenomena take on systemic forms, these rules are simultaneously subordinated to the system and are realized in coordination with the morphological system. At the next stage, it must be admitted, the rules for phenomena preserve and even intensify their relationship to the system; in addition, however, they conflict with other phonological rules, i.e., with elements of the old phonological system. Thus there arises within the phonological plane a struggle over the reflexes of the cluster *oje*, with a number of different — phonological, morphological, and, at the same time, even territorial — modifications (cf. *dobré* : *dobró, mé* : *moje, vevoda* : *vojevoda*, etc.). The morphological plane, up till now playing an inhibiting role, gets into the act as an active factor with equal rights. Even this plane can provide an incentive for contraction, especially in the case of an equilibrium of phonological forces, cf. especially the development of *oje*. Even within the plane there is a struggle taking place between elements of the old and the new quality, between the old system and the rising system of contrahends, in which, in an equilibrium of forces between the phonological and the morphological planes, there is produced, besides the SYNCHRONIC CATEGORY OF THE PLANE, also a definitely DIACHRONIC CATEGORY beyond the plane, i.e., the OPPOSITION OF THE OLD AND THE NEW SYSTEM, in which the new system represents the category of contrahend both in phonology and in morphology. This category definitely acquires a systematically dynamic character, penetrating at this stage to the morphological system. After this stage, the stage of equilibrium, the ascendancy of the morphological plane continues, until in the last stage morphological factors are the requirement for contraction. The final stage is, to a certain degree, a recapitulation of the beginning, for it is one of spontaneous change. Continuity with the new phonological and morphological category of contrahend, based on preceding stages, can however in no case be avoided. The fact that this contraction fully coincides with the contraction territory leaves us no room for doubt.

2.3 The typological and phasic characteristics of the complex process of contraction set forth in this chapter will be the basis for a course of action for investigation in this part of the book. Table 5 will serve as a synoptical summary of this chapter and at the same time as an introduction to the following chapters (the names of the stages are designated according to their characteristic features as cited in this chapter):

Stage	Abbr.	Formal Conditions	System Participation		Chap.
			Phono-logical	Morpho-logical	
1. Primary	P	$A^1 = A^2 = I$	—	—	VI
2. Phono-logical	F	$A^1 = A^2$	$+$	$(+)$	VII
3. Morphono-logical	MF	$A^1 = A^2$	$+$	$+$	VIII
4. Morphono-logical	M	$A^1 \quad A^2$	$(+)$	$+$	IX
5. Morpholo-gized	MM	—	—	$+$	X
6. Jer	J	$A^1 = ь(ъ)$	$(—)$	$(—)$	XI

TABLE 5

In the column "System Participation", the symbols $+/-$ mark presence/absence of participation, the symbol $(+)$ non-participation of negative, inhibiting factors, i.e., the presence of only positive factors, the symbol $(—)$ non-participation of positive factors, i.e., the presence of only negative factors.

The term "stage" is a chronological, diachronic expression. Besides this, the expression "contraction" is used, i.e., primary contraction, phonological contraction, etc., if type characteristics and synchronic characteristics are being stressed. This expression we include in the term "stage".

CHAPTER VI

PRIMARY CONTRACTION

1. TOWARD A DEFINITION OF CONTRACTION; ON THE ORIGIN OF CONTRACTION

1.0   Primary contraction was delimited by formula (4.3). The causes of its rise were investigated in the pertinent section, cf. IV/3.

1.1   Disregard of the system, as we have pointed out in IV/3.3, is not trivial, but is a symptom of a counter-systemic process.

2. RULES OF REALIZATION AND THEIR TERRITORY

2.1   Contraction is realized without exception, cf. IV/3.3.

2.2   For T in (4.3), it is valid that

$$T^+\text{ıI}\text{ı} \; - \; T^+\text{ī} \tag{6'}$$

that is, the property of frontness or of the lack of frontness of the preceding T is not changed by contraction, cf. further (12) in XII.

2.2.1   This means that $i//\acute{y}$ become variants of one phoneme ī.

2.3   It is to be assumed that P expands compactly over the whole contraction territory. However, concrete corroboration or modification of this thesis must be the subject of further research.

3. CONSEQUENCES AND CONCLUSION

3.0   As do the majority of cases with surface motives, P has as its result the formal (surface) destruction of the system. If underlying interferences are called therapeutic (centrifugal) then these interferences (coming from the surface), which are, after all, a normal precursor of the therapeutic processes, can be termed traumatic (centripetal) processes.

3.1   On the surface these changes of the phonological plane are manifested by the following results: Interference with the original prosodic systems, interference with accent and intonation in specific, stipulated proportions as against quantity, i.e., a new type of quantity, weakening of the principle of syllabic harmony, cf. (6), and the fusion of i, y into one "phoneme", cf. 2·2.1.

3.2   On the surface there appears the following change of the morphological plane: P destroys the boundaries between morphemes IV/3.3.

3.3   Despite these surface changes, the underlying system has preserved its original form, the proportion

$$\bar{\text{I}} : \text{III} \qquad\qquad (6\text{''})$$

represents the ratio between the surface and the underlying system, after the implementation of P.

3.4   We call this contraction "primary" because it launches the complex process of contraction and yet is not a bearer of systemic changes. This is only an empirical stage, i.e., changes have only a surface form, without consequences for the underlying system. It is an initial stage, preparing the ground for the mediation of contraction to the system proper through the superficial level.

CHAPTER VII

PHONOLOGICAL CONTRACTION

1. DEFINITION OF CONTRACTION; RISE OF CONTRACTION

1.0   We consider generalization (4.3) to be the source of phonological contraction for every A; phonological contraction, therefore, is realized for the condition

$$A^1 = A^2 \qquad (7')$$

For generalization (7'), see VIII/1.2.2, (7).

1.1   Here, of course, it was no longer a matter of superficial external interference, it was a matter of a systemic process manifested through the surface level.

1.2   Being a systemic process, it does not occur in disregard of the system, as was the case with P. There are a number of cases in which there are no morphological grounds for contraction, as *staja, krájati* in Czech.

1.3   The designation "phonological" does not mean, therefore, that morphological factors could not cooperate. The contracted forms *pěší* < *pěšьjь, pešiji* could attract such forms as *pěšaja, pěšeje, pěšějě*, especially because the form *peší*, with the rise of F, belonged only to the surface, while in the underlying system only uncontracted forms occurred, so that it could serve as the formal model for generalization (4.3) in (7').

1.4   Morphological motives here functioned as a useful, but not however, indispensable factor, for contraction occurs even in morphologically unmotivated cases such as *neje* > *ně*, *ne jeter ъ* > *něter ъ* and also in cases of the type *lajati* > *láti* (in the central region), cf. VII/4.

2. RULES OF REALIZATION AND THEIR TERRITORY

2.1.0   Contraction is realized only in those cases where there are no strong morphological restraints. Further investigation of differences in the development of the infinitive type *lajati* >

Czech, Upper Sorbian, partly Slovenian *láti/* otherwise *lajati* (cf. Table 3, in II/2.5) would show the growing influence of morphology on the territory beyond the focus, to which the development spread later.

2.1.1 The question arises as to whether contraction is not realized everywhere and whether "uncontracted" forms are not in fact partly restitutions, cf. Shevelov 1964, 525f. There is here, however, a difference between P and F. The consequences of P, and this is true also of its destructive part, survive into the historical period; with F this is not so. This difference of phenomena has its basis in the diversity of characteristics of both stages: the first stage is superficial and consequently violates (actually ignores) the system, the second is formed as systemic. It is precisely by systemicness that the territorial differences *láti/ lajati* can be better explained on the basis of 2.1.0.

2.1.2 That means that F begins to form where phonological and morphological ratios are most favorable for it. Later, when phonological motivation itself is already sufficiently strong, it can dominate even in cases of the type *lajati > láti,* where there are certainly not, however, extreme morphological constraints. On the basis of VII/1, it is possible, therefore, to formulate the internal chronology of F thus:

Phase	Type of change	Systemic conditions (+ positive, — negative)
I. 1.	*pěšaja > pěšá . . . pěšeje > pěšě* *dobraja > dobrá . . .*	+ M! (*pěšьjь, pěšiji >*) *pěší* + M! *dobrý*
II. 2.	*ne jeterъ > něterъ* *neje > ně*	none
3.	*lajati > láti/lajati*	+ F! *pěšá, dobrá* — M! *laješь* (Pres. tense) — M! *vějati*
4.	*staja > N*	the whole paradigm

Explanatory notes: I. Phase with primary phonetic motives
II. Phase without these motives
M! Morphological motivation
F! Phonological motivation

The territorial disunity in phase 3 was the beginning of a significant disintegration of contraction territory: whereas on West Slavic territory contraction reformed both the phonological and the morphological systems, on South Slavic territory it was realized in morphological objectives, cf. the following stages, further cf. XIII, especially 4.6, and XVIII/1, especially 1.2ff.

2.1.3 That counter-systemic interferences are in essence eliminated does not mean that all "uncontracted" forms are necessarily primary. It may be a matter of restitution in a new situation (before the deep structure had been affected), cf., e.g., Stanislav 1958, 502 passim, or at least partially, it may be a question of the consequences of the integration of various dialects into one language, viz., Polish.

2.2 For T it is equally valid that

$$T^+A1IA2 \rightarrow T^+A \qquad (7")$$

cf. (6) together with VI/2.2.

2.3 The problem of the relationship of contrahends to the consequent quality of the contract is alleviated by the fact that both contrahends are identical, consequently the contract must also be identical as to quality. For the reflex $\acute{e}$ $\langle eje//\check{c}j\check{e}$ it can be noted at this point that it is a matter of the same neutralization as in i $\langle bjb//iji$. On the difference between the two cases see below.

2.4 In principle, contraction is realized over the entire contraction territory, however, it is realized with greater intensity at the focus and in the central region, while on the periphery more morphological constraints are in evidence.

3. CONSEQUENCES AND CONCLUSION

3.0 The rise of phonological contraction as a systemic process progressed to a qualitative turning point in the development of contraction. This turning point influenced its entire future course and its consequences.

3.1 Whereas in P only the level of phenomena was affected phonological contraction penetrated through this level to the underlying system and directly to the phonological plane. Though, however, it established the contract as a phonological category in the first place, it affected the morphological plane as well.

3.2 The rise of the opposition Ā : AIA in the underlying system destroys the possibility of interpreting Ā as AIA. The element Ā becomes phonologically relevant; there arises a new phonological category, cf. 3.1.

3.3 Owing to the rise of this opposition the morphological segmentability of forms as *krý*, (*kyjъ* >) *ký* has been weakened, yet still capable of future (often 500 years later) restitution. However other forms contracted in P as *dobrý, strýc, kostí,* (*listъji* >) *listí* never restituted the original form, and this established the contract ı as an underlying unit. With this F brings an underlying tendency toward the replacement of polymorphemic (agglutinative and analytical) forms by synthetic forms.

3.4 The forms of imperfect as (*volaachъ, viděachъ* >) *voláchъ, viděchъ* which originally had not been associated with contraction (cf. II/3) are now interpreted as possessing contracts *á, ě,* identical with those in *dobrá, pěšě*.

3.5 The first great systemic shift appears on the horizon: a number of forms of the "hard" definite adjectives and majority of the forms of the "soft" definite adjectives already possess contracts. It is only a question of time before a structurally new declension, the adjectival declension, will definitely have arisen from the compound declension. In the central region the rise of this declension leads even farther, to the suppression of the nominal adjectival declension.

3.6 Not even the change *lajati* > *láti* (Present *lajǫ*) is without morphological consequences: this type approximates the types *kryti, kryjǫ; piti, pьjǫ; spěti, spějǫ*.

3.7 There arises a new form for the negative form of the verb *byti* in the third person singular: *ně̆*.

3.8 The first stage of the systemic part of the process of contraction is an entirely organic stage in which obviously phonological considerations are carried through. Phonology is, that is to say, directly able to accept phonetic changes into its own system. The contrahend, a hitherto surface fact, becomes a component of the phonological level. Surface conditions are brought into harmony with the phonological system. Hence this stage is termed the "phonological". As a systemic process, it also utilizes morphological factors; however, for the realization of its intentions, morphological factors are not necessary, cf. 2.1.2 and phase 2, for, in the period when it is strong enough, it can even suppress them, cf. phase 3.

CHAPTER VIII

MORPHONOLOGICAL CONTRACTION

1. The definition of contraction; the rise of contraction

1.0 A new phase in the process of contraction is the application of formula (4'), IV/1.5, to cases of the type $A^1 \cong A^2$. This definition satisfies if we explain the expression $A^1 \cong A^2$.

1.1 This expression we call a requirement of the direct contiguity of contrahends.

1.2.0 The precontraction vocalic system at the introduction of I can be formulated thus (cf., e.g., Komárek 1962, 23):

$$\text{I} \qquad\qquad u$$
$$ę \qquad e \qquad o \qquad ǫ$$
$$ě \qquad a$$

This system in a table, when we designate, in order of each vowel, on the horizontal level: a = 0, 1, 2, 3, 4 5; on the vertical level: b = 1, 2, 3, has the following form:

a \ b	0	1	2	3	4	5
1		I			u	
2	ę		e	o		ǫ
3			ě	a		

TABLE 6

The vowel ę we shall designate by a = 0, because in West Slavic languages it enters into contraction only in exceptional circumstances; in South Slavic languages it expands into one further category, i.e., forms of the genitive singular feminine.

60

1.2.1 The requirement of immedite proximity can be represented, with reference to table 6, thus:

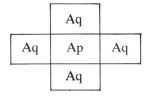

TABLE 6'

where Ap $=$ A1/A2 and Aq is the complement of Ap.

This schema, applied, e.g., to Ap $= e,$ has the following form::

	0	1	2	3	4	5
1		ı			u	
2	ę		e	o		ǫ
3			ě	a		

TABLE 6"

so that Aq $= o, \text{ě},$ i.e., the vowels immediately adjacent to e.

According to tables 6', 6", contraction can, therefore, be realized in the following cases:

e $=$ A1 1. *ejo* nonexistent, for *o* never follows *j*

2. *ejě* $>$ *ě́* West Slavic *našejě* $>$ *našě́*

e $=$ A2 3. *oje* $>$ *é/ó* *dobroje* $>$ *dobré/dobró*

4. *ěje* $>$ *ě́* *uměješь* $>$ *umě́šь*

1.2.2 Now we express, according to table 6:

1) A $=$ [a,b], i.e., e.g., ě $=$ [2,3], *u* $=$ [4,1], etc.

2) A1 $=$ [a1,b1], A2 $=$ [a2,b2]

3) e $=$ a/b; e1 $=$ a1/b1; e2 $=$ a2/b2; e', e1', e2' are the complements of e, e1, e2, i.e., if

e1 $=$ a1, then e1' $=$ b1; if e2 $=$ b2, then e2' $=$ a2, etc.

Now we shall define the conclusive difference D arithmetically thus:

$$|e1 - e2| + |e1' - e2'| = D \qquad (6)$$

where the uprights $|\ldots|$ signify absolute value.

The expression $A1 = A2$ is valid for $A1$, $A2$ with the conclusive difference

$$D = 1 \qquad (8)$$

Formula (8) defines the requirement of immediate proximity. Expression 1 here designates, according to table 6':

1) the same column, i.e., $a1 = a2$, and direct proximity in the row, i.e., $|b1 - b2| = 1$, or

2) the same row, i.e. $b1 = b2$, and direct proximity in the column, i.e., $|a1 - a2| = 1$.

Analogously, formula (7') in VII/1.0 can be expressed as

$$D = O \qquad (7)$$

1.2.3 As we see from tables 6 and 6', only the vowels $a, o, \check{c}, e$ can be in an immediate proximity in which it is valid that $A2 = o$. The following contracting clusters are realized: *oja, ejě, ěje, eja,* cf. 1.2.1.

1.3 Because, according to 1.1 and 1.2, this contraction is realized on the basis of definite phonological rules, we assume that phonological factors cooperated in the rise of this contraction, that is to say, that the requirement $A1 = A2$ was expanded even to the requirement $A1 \cong A2$. Proof of phonological factors are, for example, the contracted forms *pojasъ > pásъ, dobrějemь > dobrémь,* in which in the first instance, morphological motives are excluded, in the second instance, paralyzed, cf. 1.8; similarly also *uměješь > uměšь,* cf. 1.7.

1.4 In this stage of contraction, however, morphological motives, which, in the preceding stage, formed a sufficiently strong base to influence the development, gradually gain the upper hand.

1.5 The adjectives, which built up an entire system of contraction forms, cf. VII/3.4, continue in their advance. According to the form *pěšě* form *dobroje* contracts to *dobré.* With the aid of phonological factors the form *dobrějemъ* contracts to *dobrěmъ*, cf. 1.3.

1.6 However, this adjectival paradigm developed much greater pressure on the pronominal declension. The gen. sing. fem. *pěšě* was the model for the contraction *našěje* > *našě*, *jejě* > *jě*, etc. In the central region, *moja, moje* contract to *má, mé* according to the model *dobrá, dobré*.

1.7 In the type *umēti, uměješь* > *umēšь*, we claim a model beyond the region of contracted forms, that is to say, in the type *prositi, prosišь*, which, in the present just as in the infinitive, has a stem with a thematic ending. This, of course, was not the only factor of contraction in this type. The model *prositi, prosišь* was, of course, attractive; but the type *uměješь* was, as the weaker systematically, an unproductive and numerically a considerably restricted partner in opposition to the productive, noticeably frequent type *dělati, dělaješь*. There were here also the uncontracted types *spěti, spěješь, láti/lajati, laješь*. Consequently, the two morphological systems came into conflict. It is clear that contraction would not have been realized without phonological motives. However, the quoted type *spěti, spěješь* did not contract, though there existed for it the same PHONOLOGICAL requirements. Again, there did not exist for it a morphological model of the type *prositi, prosišь*, c.f. XI.

The interplay between the surface and underlying system can be demonstrated as follows: the opposition

    I.   *prosi-(ti)/prosi-(šь)* : II. *umē-(ti)/umēje-(šь)*

has in the underlying system the dissimilar form

    I.   *pros-i-/pros-i-* : II. *umē-ø-/umē-je-*

where the stem-forming affix is equivalent to

    in I. *-i-/-i-*

    in II. *-ø-/-je-*

so that *-ě-* in *umē-* is a word-forming affix.

What role, therefore, could the type *prositi* have played in the contraction *uměješь* > *umēšь*? The solution is instructive. The primary differentiation means that, before these types were correlated in the system, these differences had to be overcome outside it, conseqently on the surface level. As soon as contraction had been phonetically realized, therefore, the systemic association *pros-i-(šb)* : *um-ě́-(šb)* was immediately realizable.

Thus the demonstrated primariness of the surface (phonetic) process makes the description of the changes in this stage accurate: the phonetic relationships of the contrahends were still close enough (this obviously concerns the pair *e-ě* in the first series in comparison with, e.g., *o-a*) that in this generally favorable situation the act of contraction could be realized even phonetically (cf. 1. of phase F, VII/2.1.2). Of course, the concrete morphological situation was an instance in which phonetic changes would really be realized in the system and be preserved as systemic changes.

1.8 Here it is in place to call attention to why the morphological motives adduced in 1.5 were not sufficient for the development *dobrějemь* > *dobrémь*. In the form *dobřěji*, i.e., dat./loc. sing. fem. adj., the contrahends *ě, i* did not contract. Even if in the dat./loc. sing. fem. we started not from the form *dobrě-ji*, but from *dobrě-jeji*, then, according to MF, the reflex would be *ěje* > *ě́*; but this contract nevertheless does not contract with the following *i*, cf. Vážný 1962, 113, Trávníček 1935, 371, Klemensiewicz et al. 1964, 333, as preserved intervocalic *j* clearly attests. The form *dobřěji* might be contracted in view of the small degree of affinity of the contrahends up to the morphological stage, when all phonological stimuli were eliminated. Why were morphological factors, especially such strong factors as almost the whole feminine paradigm, and why, in the outcome of MM, was the fully contracted paradigm of all genders insufficient for the contraction of this form? Because the morphological requirement of hard adjectives contained in itself the hardness of the final stem consonant. But the stage of contraction, which is used exclusively as a tool for the realization of the intentions of the morphological plane, was absolutely powerless against the softness of the preceding consonants. It is possible, it must be admitted, to object that morphology accepts the correlation of this sort of softness (cf. *gora:gor'ě*); but this objection is based on a misunderstanding. Morphology is able to accept an alternation from the lower "more superficial" planes, i.e., from the phonetic or the phonological planes, and, from the synchronic point of view, to exhibit it as a component of its inventory (cf. *dobrý* : *dobří*, in which only the opposition *r* : *r'* is relevant) but it is unable to produce it as an active morphological process. Thus, it is necessary to grasp the thesis that morphological factors were paralyzed in the forms *dobrějemь, dobrěji* and that positive presence in the form *dobrějemь* — or negative absence — in the form *dobrěji* — of phonological factors in the corresponding stage of contraction arbitrated the further development.

1.9 In the central region, i.e., in the region in which the process *lajati > láti* was realized in F, the contraction *sějati > s'áti* also occurred. The contingent lesser spread of the contracted type *láti* in Polish we attribute to secondary dialectical influences.

2. Realization rules and their territory

2.1.0 This contraction is realized in cases where there are no systemic barriers to it; at the same time, phonological and morphological intentions may differ.

2.1.1 The chief obstacle for contraction languages in the realization of contraction is the principle of harmony of syllables which rejects *-é* variants. It is possible to distinguish three degrees of intensity of assertion:

1. The focus overrode all phonological barriers; the change *vojevoda > vévoda* is not morphologically motivated. Certain Slovenian dialects exhibit the same change, which indicates close proximity to the focus.

2. In the central region, but with extensions as far as the periphery (Lower Sorbian, North Polish, Serbo-Croatian dialects), contraction is carried out with strong morphological motives, as in *dobroje > dobré*. Much weaker morphological motives are carried out only in the central region: *mojego > mégo*.

3. In some parts of the periphery — Central Slovak, Štokavian — no morphological motives brought about the rise of *-é*. The possibility is not ruled out that also in other parts of the periphery where the form *dobré* is attested it may be a matter of newer influences from the central region.

The chronological process was, of course, reversed. First, in the period when MF has to begin to be realized, requirement (8) comes up against the principle of harmony. Thus there come into conflict two phonological subsystems: a new one, represented by the requirement cited, and an old one, represented by harmony. The morphological system, which has already acquired enough strength to be able to encroach actively upon the contraction process, comes to the aid of contraction. The barriers to *dobroje,* in which change is most strongly motivated, fall first. Next in line come cases in which change is not immediately motivated, but is merely freely motivated — on immediate and free morphological conditions see IX/1.3 — and cases like *mojego* contract. Finally, the change of *oje* is realized even without the aid of morphological factors, as in *vojevoda.* It is entirely comprehensible that the earlier the change arose, the greater expansion it achieved. The correspondence among intensity of motives, chronology, and territorial extent is here entirely explicit.

2.1.2 The breaking of the barrier of the old principle of harmony to a great extent influenced the rise of the softness correlation of consonants. It seems that in this stage differences within the contraction region intensified: on the periphery, where $^-é$ was not carried through, perhaps this correlation did not arise at all — the change of the type *šějati > s'áti* is here unrealized and, moreover, later stages of contraction, which carry through morphological interests, could undertake nothing here, c.f. e.g., *dobrujemu > dobrómu.* The weakening of the intensity of contraction on the periphery has, therefore, not only no quantitive character, but also no qualitative, systemic character.

2.1.3 Analogously to F (in VII/2.1.2), it is possible to stipulate the following phases in MF:

Phase	Type of change	Systemic relationships (=> secondary systemic association)
I.	1. *umĕješ > umčšь* *našejĕ > našé*	⇒ M. *prosišь* ⇒ M. *pĕšč*
	2. *pojasъ > pásъ* *moja >* Czech, Slovak Slovenian, Polish *má*/all N	∅ +M. *dobrá* —M. stem *moj-*
II.	3. *dobroje > dobré*/Centr., Slovak, Štokavian N	—F. lack of *é* and of the opposition T'e : T$^-$e +M. *dobrý : pčší* *dobrá : pĕšá* *dobrá : pĕšč*

II.	4. *sějati* > West Slavic *s'áti*/South Slavic N	—F. lack of the opposition T' : T +M. *láti* —M. *lajati*
	5. *vojevoda* > Czech, Slovenian *vévoda*/the rest N	—F. lack of *e* and of the opposition T' : T⁻e violated in 3.
	moje > Czech, Slovenian *mé*/all N	—F. the same +M. *dobré* —M. stem *moj*-
	mojego, mojemu . . . > Czech, Slovenian *mégo, mému* . . ./others N	—F. the same +M. new possessive stem *m*-; cf. *m-á, m-é*

For explanatory notes see VII/2.1.2.

2.2 For the softness character of T, (7") is valid; cf. however, 1.8.

2.3 For the determination of the quality of the contract, $\bar{A} = A^2$ is valid. If this requirement cannot be realized, contraction is not realized (periphery). This requirement is valid also for the cluster *ěje* > *ě*, cf. VII/2.3.

2.4 Contraction is realized irregularly as to territory. Only the cases *ěje, ejě* > *ě*, where the qualitative principle $\bar{A} = A^1/A^2$ can be applied, are consistently valid for the whole territory, cf. VII/2.3. It is possible, therefore, to assume that it is precisely these cases, together with cases of the type *pojasъ* > *pásъ*, which represented the original cases of morphonological contraction, for it is precisely the pair of contrahends in the vertical direction — following table 6 — which were homogenous in relation to a preceding T and could not, therefore, provoke a conflict between the new and the old systemic requirements. In the horizontal direction contraction was delayed and was not realized at all on the periphery.

2.5 MF contraction, therefore, to a certain extent, also fell apart chronologically into two types or phases. In the first phase, phonological factors dominate; in the second phase, morphological factors are carried through to an ever increasing degree. The transition from phonological motivation to predominance, to the extent of total dominance, of morphological factors was realized precisely in this stage.

3. CONSEQUENCES

3.0 The rise of MF means the retreat of the qualitative condition $A = A^1/A^2$; the condition $A = A^2$ asserts itself. Against the preceding stage, in the second phase of MF, morphological motives assert themselves, which leads to a new systemic phenomenon — conflict between systems.

3.1 On the basis of 2.4. it is to be assumed that this stage asserts itself through the phase ěje/ejč > ě́, i.e., in cases where the rule $A = A^1/A^2$ was applicable. But according to VIII/1, we assume $D = 1$ for these cases, so that a further phase of this stage is only a generalization of this rule.

3.2 From this, however, arises the problem of the quality of the contract, hitherto automatically decided by the identity of the two contrahends. Why does a regressive tendency, i.e., the quantitative principle $A = A^2$, assert itself?

3.3 The adjectival paradigm develops only in details. The form (dobroje >) dobré, however, expressly fills out the nominative pairs dobrý : pěší, dobrá : pčšá, dobré : pěšě́ and at the same time lays the ground work for the formation of indirect cases in further phases (dobrajego > dobrégo, etc.). However, the influence of this paradigm on the pronominal declension, which precisely in this stage begins to change under its influence, most intensively in the central region, is conspicuous.

3.4 The most substantial occurrence is, however, the first strong incursion into the region of conjugation. Following the model of type prosišь there arises the new present type uměšь. This development, unlike other morphological changes, occurs very compactly. It does not penetrate e.g. to the peripheral Polish dialects, cf. umiejesz, Klemensiewicz et al. 1964, 56; on the other hand, however, it does show a tendency to expand to the transperiphery.

3.5   Because of this change, the types *uměšь* : *spěješь* differ sharply, c.f. on this XVI.

3.6   In the infinitive stem there appear relatively small, territorially restricted changes. In the central region, the infinitive *sějati* contracts to *s'áti,* to a lesser extent, also *stojati* > *státi.*

4.   CONCLUSION

4.0   This stage is called morphonological because the phonological and morphological systems come not only into combination, but also into opposition. This duality of motivation also has its own chronological and territorial form: in the initial phase, still bound to the preceding F, phonological motives keep dominating and the contraction territory develops relatively integrally; in the second phase, morphological likewise make themselves felt and the contraction territory is conspicuously differentiated not only quantitatively, but also qualitatively.

4.1   The intersystemic conflict revolves around the rise of the variant -*é*. The old phonological system did not admit this variant and it yielded only gradually; it first evacuated its positions under strong morphological pressure; later, under less intensive pressure, even in the focus, whatever phonological barriers there were fell completely; the change *oje* > *é* is here realized as a phonological process, therefore, even without the support of morphological motivation. On the periphery, on the other hand, not even the strongest morphological factors asserted themselves and the contraction of this contracting cluster was not realized until after the qualitative condition $A = A^2$ had vanished.

4.2   Besides this, it is essential that at the same time conflicts arise within the systems between the elements of the old and the new qualities. In the phonological system, the conservative principle was the requirement of harmony, the progressive principle the requirement $A = A^2$. The nearer the focus, the more strongly the progressive principle is carried through.

4.3   Similar conflicts occurred also within the morphological system. The type *umčješь,* though it stands in opposition on the one hand to the type *dělaješь,* on the other hand to the type *spčješь,* is nevertheless attracted by the type *prosišь*. This conflict is solved, of course, by intervention from beyond the morphological system: phonological factors contributed to contraction. Phonological motivation played a similar deciding part in the balance of morphological factors in the contraction of the form *dobrějemъ*.

4.4 As we see from the preceding section, the most important driving force of this stage was intrasystemic conflict between conservative and progressive principles. The progressive phonological and morphological principles can unite against the conservative principles and in cases of this kind the old principle as a rule does not prevail. Thus, not intersystemic conflicts, but intrasystemic conflicts, together with intersystemic coordination, are the most essential motivating forces of this stage.

4.5 Morphonological contraction represents a qualitative breakthrough in the development of the complex of systemic contractions. There is a gradual transition from the dominance of phonology to morphological motivation. There occur profound territorial differences; in the center, the principle of harmony is in retreat after the rise of the new, contraction quantity, the deepest incursion into the old phonological system.

CHAPTER IX

MORPHOLOGICAL CONTRACTION

1. DEFINITION OF CONTRACTION; THE RISE OF CONTRACTION

1.0 This stage proceeds entirely from motives of the morphological system, which in the preceding stages built itself a sufficiently wide base of contracted forms and enabled it to take over the initiative completely. Process (7) here applies to cases of the type A1 ∼ A2.

1.1 The expression A1 ∼ A2 we shall call the requirement of indirect proximity, which, according to tables 6, 6', and 6", has the following distribution:

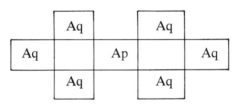

TABLE 7

If we now proceed in the manner of table 6", then, for example, for Ap = e, the following possibilites come under consideration:

$e = $ A¹ 1. *eji* $>$ *í*   *našeji* $>$ *naší*
     2. *eję* $>$ *ę́*   *našeję* $>$ *našę́* (South Slavic)
     3. *eja*   —

$e = $ A² 4. *ije* $>$ *ě̆*   *pešijemь* $>$ *pešě̆mь*
        ьje $>$ *ě̆*   *čьje* $>$ *čě̆, čьjego* $>$ *čě̆go* . . .
     5. *ěje*   —
     6. *aje* $>$ *á/ě̆,*   *dělaješь* $>$ *dě̆lášь, pešajego*
        often also *é*   *pě̆šě̆go* (*dobrajego* $>$ *dobrégo*)

Initially, this requirement can be expressed as

$$D = 2 \tag{9}$$

which states that the Aq position is in immediate proximity to the position immediately adjacent to the Ap position, however, it is not Ap (cf. table 7):

1.2 All cases, negative as well as positive, are morphologically motivated. Thus, e.g., the contraction *pěšijemь* > *pěšěmь* is motivated by the contracted forms of the adjectival paradigms. On the other hand, the cases *kryješь, šiješь, pьješь,* with the same forms of contrahends, do not contract; they adhere to the general morphological models *laješь, spěješь, čuješь* . . Cases like *ostrьje* do not contract, having in addition motives both within the paradigm — cf. *ostrьja, ostrьju* — and also in parallel paradigms — *mor'e, mor'a* . . . etc.

1.3.0 For the formulation of the actions of morphological factors we use the concept MORPHOLOGICAL CONDITIONING, which will be explained in subsequent paragraphs.

1,3.1 In our considerations hitherto, it sufficed to consider morphological factors — whether positive or negative — as a whole. In the two subsequent stages, i.e., in M and MM, it is necessary to distinguish two types of factors, viz., internal and external. By internal factors we understand morphological motives within a paradigm; by external factors we understand extra-paradigmatic, but homorphous, i.e. with analogous morphological characteristics or motives. These external motives are partly direct, i.e. they have identical characteristics in form, (e.g., case, number, gender), and partly universal (i.e., correspondences between a paradigm in which a form contracts and a paradigm which contains a form with internal direct motives). Thus, for example, the form *dobroje* underwent contraction

(1) on the basis of such internal stimuli as the contracted forms *dobrý, dobrá,* etc.

(2) on the basis of such direct external stimuli as the form of the soft type *pěšč* with identical morphological characteristics,

(3) with general stimuli such as the correspondences between the hard and the soft types of adjectives — *dobrý : pěší, dobrá : pěšá,* etc., *dobrýchъ : pěšíchъ,* etc.

We designate
internal motives | In.,
external motives | Ex.,
direct external motives | ExD.,
indirect external motives | ExG.

1.3.2 Not all morphological motives have to be results of contraction. Thus, in the contraction *uměješь > umě̃šь*, the morphological motive was the model *prosišь*, which does not contain a contract.

1.3.3 The strength of the morphological conditioning is determined by the intensity of the motives; if In. or ExD. (ExG. is bound to ExD.) is lacking, we speak of FACULTATIVE CONDITIONING; if all stimuli operate simultaneously, we speak of OBLIGATORY CONDITIONING.

1.4 For morphological contraction the requirement of facultative conditioning suffices. In essence, the following cases are concerned:

Change	Conditions
1. *ije > ě̃: pěšijemь >* *pěšě̃mь* (Loc. sg. m/n)	In. *pěší, pěšě̃ . . . pěšímь . . .* ExD. *dobrěmь*, poss. *našemь* ExG. *pěší : dobrý . . .* *pěšímь : dobrýmь : našimь*
2. *ьje > ě̃:čьje,* *čьjego, čьjemь >* *čě̃, čě̃go, čě̃mь*	In. *čí, čímь (< čьjь, čьjьmь* in P) ExD. *pěšě̃(mé), pěšě̃go* (cf. 7, poss. *mégo*) . . . ExG. *čí : pěší, čímь : pěšímь*
3. *eji > í: našeji >* *naší, jeji > jí* (Dat. sg. fem.)	In. *našě̃, jě̃* ExD. *pěší* ExG. *našě̃, jě̃ : pěšě̃,* poss. *naša . . . našichъ :* *pěšá . . . pěšíchъ . . .*
4. *aje > á: dělaješь . . . >* *dělášь . . .*	In. - ExD. *umě̃šь, prosišь* ExG. *dělati : uměti, prositi*
5. *'aje > ě̃: pěšajego >* *pěšě̃go*	In. *pěší, pěšě̃ . . . pěšíchъ . . .* ExD. (*čě̃go, mégo, našego*) ExG. *pěší : čí : našь . . .*

In the central region, further:

Change	Conditions
6. *-aje* > *é*: *dobrajego* > *dobrégo*	In. *dobrý, dobré . . . dobrýchъ* ExD. *mégo, kégo* ExG. *dobrý : ký, dobré : mé, ké*
7. *ojǫ* > *ǫ*: *tojǫ, ženojǫ, tobojǫ* > *tǿ, ženǿ, tobǿ*	In. - (monosyllabicity of endings in the paradigm) ExD. *dobrǿ* ExG. *ta . . . : dobrá . . .*
8. *ojě* > *é*: *tojě* > *té*	In. Cf. 7 ExD. *našě́, jě́* ExG. *ta : naša*

On the periphery:

Change	Conditions
6'. *-oje* > *ó*: *dobroje* > *dobró*	In. *dobrý, dobrá . . . dobrýchъ* ExD. *to, ono; pěšě́, naše* ExG. *dobrý : onъ, pěší . . .* *to, ono : naše, pěšě́* *dobro : pěše*
6". *-aje* > *ó*: *dobrajego* > *dobrógo*	In. Cf. 6, but *dobró!* ExD. *togo, pěšě́go, našego* ExG. *dobró : to, pěšě́, naše*
7'. *ejǫ* > *ę́*: *našejǫ* > *našę́, jejǫ* > *ję́*	In. Cf. 7 ExD. *pěšę́* ExG. *naša : pěšá*
8'. *yję* > *ę́*: *dobryję* > *dobrę́*	In. *dobrá . . .* ExD. *pěšę́ . . .* ExG. *dobrá : pěšá . . .*

    1.5 Similarly, as positive factors operate, negative factors are also carried through. For these reasons the forms *laješь, šiješь . . . , ostrьje . . .* are not contracted. On the concrete form of their constraints, c.f. 1.2.

    1.6 The adjectival declension gained more ground on the periphery even where the preceding stage was not successful.

1.7 The pronominal paradigm is subject to changes in direct connection with the adjectival declension and outside of this connection.

1.8 Why does the cluster *ojǫ* not become contracted in some languages or, rather, dialects (Central Slovak, štokavian, South Čakavian)? In morphological contraction, the motives must have been morphological. This means that here there was no contracted form *dobrǫ́* that would have served as ExD. It may be assumed, therefore, that the absence of contraction is caused by the fact that, in a certain territory, there did not exist a form *dobrǫjǫ* for the Instrumental, but only a form *dobrojǫ*. Cf. on this XV/1.

1.9 The new conjugation system is given final shape; the pairs *uméšь : spěješь, děláśь : laješь* are definitely differentiated.

2. RULES AND TERRITORY

2.1 Contraction is realized only in the case of morphological stimuli. For contraction, facultative conditioning suffices.

2.2 For the soft character of a preceding T, requirement (7') is always valid.

2.3 For the quality Ā there is no determinative formula Ā = A2, cf. VIII/2.3, but there is morphological motivation. ExD. participates in these morphological motivations with deciding influence.

2.4 Contraction is realized spasmodically according to specific models, but the differences betwen the central region and the periphery do not deepen further. Rather, this stage seems to be, in comparison with the preceding stage, territorially more integral.

3. CONSEQUENCES

3. The substantial retreat of phonological motives receives expression in the fact that only the phonological requirement D = 2 cooperates in this phase, and that, of course, merely negatively. Whereas in F morphological factors have merely marginal functions, in this stage the relationship is reversed: phonological motivation here plays a marginal, purely negative role.

3.1 A single, final step remains to the adjectival declension for a definitive historical form.

3.2 The pronominal paradigm is given motion.

3.3 Contraction changes in conjugation are completed.

4. CONCLUSION

4.1 There is not much that remains from the phonological requirements. The most important factor is the retreat of the qualitative principle $\bar{A} = A_2$ and its replacement by morphological considerations, even to the end that $\bar{A}$ need have nothing at all in common with the contrahends as to quality — cf. *dobrógo,* cf. analogies with East Slavic forms of the type (*dobrago* >)*dobrogo,* in which the process $a > o$ was motivated by the pronominal declension, cf. *t-ogo, k-ogo, sam-ogo,* etc.. But here again there is a striking difference: the South Slavic form was linked to the system *dobró : pěšě, dobrógo : pěšégo,* etc., with contracted forms, as one of the relevant features of the contract, namely quantity, indicates.

4.2 Intersystem conflicts and coordination are weakened with the retreat of phonological motives. Conflicts within the morphological system have, of course, free rein.

4.3 The systems that did not accept the variant ⁻é must retreat to another position, admitting a hitherto unknown element, long ō. Because they did not admit the softness correlation in MF, they can no longer properly carry it through, for in this phase it is already a question of the realization of solely morphological intentions.

4.4 Morphological contraction unifies and systematizes the morphological consequences of the preceding phases and impresses the by now historical form of the language onto the majority of morphological categories — adjectives, pronouns, verbs.

CHAPTER X

MORPHOLOGIZED CONTRACTION

1. Definition of contraction; the rise of contraction

1. The purpose of this stage is the filling in of the gaps that have remained in the paradigms after the preceding stages. They are regulated, of course, by rule (7), but the relationship of the contrahends, hitherto a deciding criterion for the individual stages of contraction, is here entirely indifferent, so that it is valid that

$$D > 2 \qquad\qquad (10)$$

1.1 The laxer the phonological conditions are, the stricter are the morphological constraints. For the realization of contraction in this stage, obligatory conditioning (cf. IX/1.3.3) is necessary.

1.2 The following cases in particular are concerned:

Changes	Conditions
1. *ьja, ьje*, . . . *á, é* : *čьja*, (*čьjejě* >) *čьjě* > *čá, čě*	In. Cf. IX/1.4.2 ExD. *pěšá, pěšě* . . . ExG. Cf. IX/1.4.2
2. *'uje* > *ě* : *pěšujemu* > *pěšěmu*	In. Cf. IX/1.4.5 ExD. *čěmu, našemu* ExG. C. IX

In the central region further:

Changes	Conditions
3. *⁻uje* > *é* : *dobrujemu* > *dobrému*	In. Cf. IX/1.4.6 ExD. *mému, kému* ExG. Cf. IX
4. *ejǫ, ьjǫ* > *ǫ́* : *dušejǫ, našejǫ* > *dušǫ́, našǫ́* *kostьjǫ* > *kost'ǫ́*, *čьjejǫ* > *čějǫ́* > *čǫ́*	In. *dušč, naše* . . . ExD. *ženǫ́, pěšǫ́, tǫ́* ExG. *dušč, našě* . . . : *žena, pěšě, té* . . .

Changes	Conditions

5. *oji* > *ý* :
   toji > *tý* (Dat. sg. f.)
	In. *ta, té, tǫ́*
	ExD. *naší, pěší*
	ExG. *ta : naša, pěšá; té :*
	   našé, pěšé
	Cf. IX/1.4.8

6. *yje* > *é* :
   dobryjě > *dobré*
 	
In the focus further:
7. *oji* > *ý*
   mojïmь, mojichъ >
   týmь, mýchъ
	
	In. *má, mé, mégo*
	ExD. *dobrýmь, dobrýchъ* . . .
	ExG. *má . . .mégo : dobrá . . .*
	   dobrégo . . .

8. *ěji* > *í* ⇒ *eji* *ý*
   (*mojeji* >) *méji* >
   mý (Dat. sg. f.)
	In. *má,* Gen. *mé* . . .
	ExD. *tý, čí, pěší, naší* . . .
	ExG. *má : ta, čá* . . .
	   mé : té, čé

In the periphery further:

3'. *uje* > *ó*   Cf. IX/1.4.6"
   dobrujemu > *dobrómu*

   1.3 Contrariwise, contraction was not realized for lack of positive motives (facultative conditioning) or because of negative motives (designated by x):

Changes	Conditions

1. *uje*
   kupuješь, bojuješь > N
	In. -
	ExD. *prosišь, uméšь*
	ExG. *prositi, uměti :*
	   kupovati, bojevati
	Cf. XII/2

2. *ěji, oji*
   dobrěji (Dat. sg. f.)
   moji (Nom.pl.m.) > N
 	
On the periphery further:
3. *oji*
   mojichъ > N
	
	In. -
	ExD. *dobrýchъ*
	ExG. *moja, moje, mojego :*
	   dobrá, dobró, dobrógo

For similar reasons we assume the absence of contraction in this stage for cases like *ulьja, ostrьja, sodьja; panьjě* . . . *panьjǫ,* etc.

1.4 This stage of contraction had to fill in with contracted forms those positions in the paradigms in which in the preceding stages contraction did not occur. This process (though of course empirically with the phonetic reflexes) has, therefore, a purely systemic, morphological impulse and the outcome is that it completes the rise of contraction paradigms, cf. XIV.

1.5 The process of the rise of the adjectival declension is completed in the whole region. The long vowel, having a contract as its mark, is generalized (the single exception is *dobrěji,* cf. VIII/1.8).

1.6 The pronominal declension likewise acquires its historical form. Territorial differences are already brought about by the preceding stages and by the difference West Slavic -*ě* : South Slavic -*ę*.

1.7 In conjugation we take into account a minor (uncited) change *prьjati* > *pr'áti,* which was realized in accordance with *s'áti* (with agrement of the present, cf. *prěješь* : *sěješь*).

1.8 The substantive in essence avoided the whole process of contraction. Only in a part of contraction territory do we observe this process in the Instr. sing. fem. But this has no real relevance for declension as a whole.

1.9 Somewhat more complex for reconstruction is the development of a nominal declension of the adjectival type *tretí*. In the historical period we can state its full integration with the adjectival declension *pěší*. When, however, did this integration occur? It is certain that P had already introduced a series of agreements between the two declensions, e.g., Nom. sing. and pl. masc., Loc., Instr. sing. masc., neut. We here proceed from the presupposition that the consequences of P, taken by themselves, did not fundamentally influence morphological development, i.e., could not be a morphological motivation. This also has a bearing upon such types as *úlí, ostrьje,* with which the nominal type *tretí* is in full agrement. If the nominal declension of the adjective is realized as an independent paradigm agreeing with the declension of *úlí,* etc., there is for M here no presupposition.

2. RULES AND TERRITORY

2.1 Contraction is completely subordinate to the needs of morphology. This extreme character of contraction brings with it the requirement of obligatory conditioning.

2.2 For the soft character of T rule (7') (cf. VIII/2.2) remains in force.

2.3 For the quality of Ā, the form in ExD, consequently a morphological consideration, is the deciding factor.

2.4 Contraction is realized according to the demands of the individual contraction regions or languages; where in the preceding phases changes were constrained for phonological reasons, they could now be freely realized. This means a definite reapproximation of the contraction territory.

3. CONSEQUENCES AND CONCLUSION

3.0 This contraction completed the contraction systems of adjectives, of pronouns, and of conjugation in its details.

3.1 This stage is called "morphologized" because the process of contraction is fully realized in the intentions of morphology, i.e., without regard for other planes. Therefore, morphology is governed by its own requirements wholly without constraint, exactly as, at one time at the beginning of the whole process of contraction, F was. These two stages, representing, in a certain sense, the two poles of the process, have, at the same time, the common feature of sovereignty of decision.

3.2 Even this process, of course, must have on the surface, features of contraction, i.e., a contract must arise, though not new phonemes or variants. Apart from changes in a contracting cluster, T^+ remains intact; no morphological changes influence it.

3.3 This phase, pursuant to 3.1, in a certain sense completes the process of contraction as a whole; at the same time, it closes the systematically motivated stage of the process. That is to say, all possibilities for realization are exhausted, from the phonetic through the phonological by transitional stages all the way to the extremely morphological, i.e., MM. From the surface, therefore, the process penetrates deeper in a further stage underlying system where, at first, the phonological plane, which is able to select models directly from the surface, i.e. from the plane of phonetics, is dominant. There arises a new, progressive principle — the quantity of the contrahend — which comes into conflict with the old prosodic principles. In a further stage (on the deeper level), in which the morphological plan becomes an active participants in the process, there arise not only intersystemic conflicts, but also intrasystem conflicts and, at the same time, intrasystem coordination, directed toward the enforcement of new principles. To these principles also belongs the first encroachment on the system of the harmony of syllables. But in the course of these conflicts and cooperation the possibilities of phonology are gradually exhausted, whereas the morphological system builds new positions in the paradigm, from which, after final domination of the paradigm, it proceeds to the construction of the contraction paradigm as a whole and of the contract as a morphological category. This aim culminates precisely in this final systemic stage of contraction. A single flectional category remains unaffected as a whole — the substantive.

CHAPTER XI

JER CONTRACTION

1. DEFINITION OF CONTRACTION; THE RISE OF JER CON-
TRACTION

1.0 Thus contraction exhausted all its possibilities without asserting itself morphologically in the substantive. In this final phase of the contraction process a mighty impulse arrives. Its original motivation is superficial and in addition is independent of contraction. This impulse nevertheless will play a fundamental role in the completion of the systemic, primarily morphological intentions of contraction. This impulse is the fall of the jers.

1.1 Jer contraction is always valid, if (4"), (7), and $A^1 = b$ ($\mathfrak{b}$) are valid. From this formulation it is obvious that it is again realized regardless of the system; but almost lacking the possibility of interfering with the phonological system (possibly only the unstable phoneme $'\acute{e}$ rises anew in the central region), in this plane it affects much more the periphery (implications for the softness correlation of consonants) it primarily affects the morphological system.

1. There can be no doubt in principle that this process stems from the process of contraction: it is realized only in contraction languages and it follows the rules of contraction.

1.3 Continuity with the preceding stages was assured by the fact that here already in the typologically earlier stages this contraction was realized, cf. *čьje* > *čě* . . . , *kostьjǫ* > *kost'ǫ* . . . , cf. IX, X. Typological differences, that is, in this epoch do not presuppose chronological differences; J could be realized at the same time as the last stages of the systemic epoch. See 2.4, 2.5.

1.4 Sometimes there is doubt whether J had spontaneous character. Obviously, changes like *pьješь* > *pěšь*, *zmьja* > *zm'á*, which are in direct contradiction to the interests of the system, are examples of spontaneous character, cf. against this *šiješь*, *kryješь* . . . , *šija, staja* . . . The fact that Polish does not have evidence for contraction of this type, cf. Klemensiewicz et al.

1964, 114, does not mean that in this language it did not exist. If Czech were attested in the same way as Polish, we would have to draw conclusions about Czech in a similar manner. Pauliny 1963, 88, meets the same objection: "With regard to the present (sic) state, the second possibility (i.e., not *bьještь* > *běštь*, but *bi-eštь* > *biještь*) is the more probable". But why does *ьje* develop now as *ě* (cf. *listě* with the corresponding reflexes in all the contraction languages), now as *i-e?* Not even different morphological conditions can lead to a vocalization of this sort. In Czech with more complete documentation, the facts, both the historical and the reconstructed, prevent the projection of later stages (*biješ*) in this way. The fact that in the other West Slavic languages we do not have data of equal antiquity, and consequently those with equal amount of information, can hardly lead us to decide about them in an utterly different manner.

2. RULES AND TERRITORY

2.1   Contraction is realized in all cases when $A^1 = $ ь.

2.2   It is qualitatively valid that $\bar{A} = A^2$, which is a known regressive principle already validated, chiefly in MF. As a new principle it appears, of course, in certain peripheral regions. This is connected with the fact that here systemic interferences are excluded; it is concretely connected with the fact that it concerns a process realized in close dependence upon the surface change of the fall of the jers.

2.3   Cases with $A^2 = $ ь represent the clusters in which a regressive, even if not systemic, but surface, change is to be considered. Forms like *ujьcь. . . , lajь, spějь . . . , mojь. . .* did not contract, though they had the same morphological motives as did the contracted forms *strýcь . . . , krý, ší . . ., dobrý, dobrá : má . . .* Regressive contraction was lost because of the weak intensity of the jers — J arose in connection with the fall of the jers, which presupposes their reduction. If not even progressive contraction is realized against systemic interests, then this attests to the exclusion of systemic, morphological influences and at the same time attests to the principle of regressive contraction always being contrary to this morphological motivation.

2.4   This observation has fundamental relevance also for the chronology of J. Contracting clusters with $A^2 = $ ь NEVER contract in MM (in M they do not apparently come into consideration). For example, the form *mojъ* is in Czech or in Slovenian the only form of the singular that ignores contraction; in all other cases, there exist at least doublets like *moja/má*. Under normal conditions, the absence of contraction in MM with regard to such strong morphological impulses (cf. in addition again the parallel declension of hard adjectives!) is absolutely excluded. This means that ъ was already in the process of extinction, that it was governed by the rules of J without regard for MM, that, therefore, J, though typologically later, chronologically overlaps MM.

2.5 This chronological continuity between J and the remaining stages also reliably explains the typological continuity: entirely the same contraction clusters were subject to M and MM as to J (cf. M: *čъje*, MM: *čъja* . . . . , *kostъjǫ*, but J:*listъje, listъja, sǫdъja* . . . *sǫdъjǫ, panъjǫ*); because J is realized at the same time, the changes in M and MM were formally and chronologically a perfect model for the changes in J.

2.6 This interpretation excludes the notion that contracting clusters with A1 = ъ developed so that this contrahend was lost. This would yield the diphthongoid concatenation IA, i.e., *ъje* > *ie*, *ъja* > *ia*, etc., as is the case in non-contraction languages. This thesis has already been abandoned and there is no need to pursue it further. Much more relevant is the objection to our interpretation arising from certain incontestible properties of the system; it presupposes that it is only a matter of compensatory lengthening. In a certain sense, we cannot object to anything as long as we conceive of contraction as a whole in this manner, i.e., that as the replacement for two short vowels there arises one long one, the contract. This interpretation is altogether welcome, for it stresses the qualitatively new phonological stage motivated by contraction, a stage refuting the original phonological system, for such certainly partially surviving quantitative oppositions as ъ : *i*, *e* : *ě* are irrelevant for this new stage; the phonemes *i, e, a* are short in opposition to the contrahends *í, ě́, á*. On the other hand, we do not assign to such a type of compensatory lengthening as is the type *bogъ* > *bóg*, for here it is a case of "the lengthening of the preceding vowel" (Klemensiewicz et al. 1964, 52, and also to examples mentioned by Komárek 1962, 33-36), in which one cannot always distinguish cases of lengthening and cases of the new acute. The length of the contract, on the contrary, is always realized, without regard for the original prosodic relationships.

3. CONSEQUENCES

3.1 In spite of its phonetic, non-systemic behavior, J develops in an entirely different way from P. This is a consequence of the preceding processes, when Ā became a new phonological and morphological category; for that reason, the results of this stage are interpreted not only on the surface, but also in the underlying system.

3.2 In the phonological system of the central region, merely marginal changes are realized. By contraction of the participle *pьjе̨* > *pе̨́* there arises in the system a new, but not very stable, element *'е̨́*. The category of contracts is rather complete quantitatively, e.g. the phoneme *ú*, up till now of low frequency — only in certain dual forms, viz., (*dobruju* >) *dobrú*, (*toju, onoju* >) *tú, onú*, (*našeju* >) *našú*, cf. XV/3.9 — is now represented in the Dat. sing. masc./neut. as *úl'ú, ostr'ú*, etc. On the periphery apparently, J affords the possibility of forming the hitherto unrealizable softness correlation of consonants; it seems that these possibilities were not sufficiently exploited; in particular, the South Slavic periphery does not exhibit any systemic consequences in its phonology even in other cases; here also, not even the quantity of the contract upset the original prosodic system, as it did in West Slavic territory.

3.3.0 In the focus, jer contraction extends even into cases with $A^1 = ъ$, where $\& = \&o$ at the same time! For example, *vь uši* > *v úši, kъ oku* > *k óku*. The condition $\& = \&i$ is, to a certain extent, bypassed by this, cf. (4"); furthermore, in the focus there arises a new phoneme *ó*, typologically already known earlier on the periphery in the forms *dobró, dobrógo*, etc. On the relevance of this Czech change to contraction see Shevelov 1964, 527.

3.3.1 Komárek 1962, 86, offers a different solution, for "the same conditions in the end obtained even for the preposition *jьz*", i.e., he presupposes an older process of a shifting of the stress from the jer (in the preposition) onto a following vowel (progressive compensatory lengthening was excluded, cf. 2.6).

Is it true that after the preposition *z* there is lengthening? If *o* were lengthened in *jьz oka* 'from the eye' it would probably have to be lengthened in the same manner in, e.g. *vъzori, vъzorati, jьzorati,* as in prefixed verbs this lengthening would be even more probable; in cases with jers in inlaut, i.e., in the initial syllable, like *kъto,* it is most probable of all. The thesis stated in Shevelov 1964 does not have these stumbling blocks.

3.4 Whereas hitherto the substantive paradigm was nearly intact, it underwent in the course of this phase of contraction changes which equal in far-reaching consequences the results of the entire preceding process in other paradigms. That is to say, there arise types with contracting endings like *úlí,* Gen. *úľá; sǫdá, paní,* Gen. *paně; ostrě,* which, particularly in the central region, are marked by considerable autonomy. It is as a result of further development that, e.g., Slovak and especially Czech elaborated this autonomy, whereas, for example, Polish had to give it up in connection with systemic changes (the loss of quantity, cf. XIV/2.6). These contracting types stand after J in the same or a similar correlation to the non-contracting types as in the case, for example, with adjectives or verbs.

3.5 The nominal declension of adjectives of the type *tretí,* which fully agreed with the paradigms of the above-mentioned substantives, develops in parallel with this system. In this way, however, it reached agreement — at least in the majority of forms — with the "compound", i.e., the now already adjectival declension of the type *pěší,* with which, in regard to its function, it had already merged in prehistoric times.

3.6 There arises the present paradigm *p'ǫ́, pěšь* . . . , the participles *pǫ́, p'ǫ́ci* . . . , but this has no support in the system, so that later it returns to the original system; following *šiju, kryju,* etc., *piju,* etc., are formed anew.

3.7 Similarly, the substantive *zm'á* changes to *zmija.*

3.8 After these findings there remains now very little that is unclear. The pronoun *čьjь* is reflected in Polish by the forms *czyj, czyja,* etc., as though here the cluster *ьj* represented *ij,* cf. Klemensiewicz et al., 114. Why here exactly? We repeat the question from 1.4. The only non-morphological reason that we can find (in *op. cit.* it is not mentioned) lies in the fact that the cases occur in inlaut. But even these cases are contracted in Polish, cf. *trьje > trze.* Also Sorbian excludes the rise of *ьj* to *ij* in the above-mentioned pronoun, cf. Upper Sorbian *čeji*, Lower Sorbian *ceji*, cf. Mucke 1891, 397. If we were to cite only Lechitic languages on the same basis, then the Polish forms would not be representative. It is obvious that in both branches it is a question of secondary forms that have been altered for certain reasons. If we consider that in both branches quantity has been lost, then the difference represented in Czech by the opposition *čeho : ččho, i.e.*, West Slavic *čego : čégo*, vanishes. Hence the innovations; in Polish, it is chiefly the nominative **czy* (cf. secondary *bijesz* etc.) which provided the starting point for them; in Sorbian the most frequent form of the stem, *če/ce-*, became their basis.

3.9 If 3.8 is generally valid, i.e., if it is valid that initial syllables with *ьj* develop the same as syllables in other positions, then cases like *prьjatelь, prьjaznь*, which contract only in Czech, Sorbian, and Slovak, still remain a mystery in Polish and South Slavic. The fact that it concerns contraction languages that have preserved the verb *prьjati* leads us to the assumption that these substantives were, in the other languages, already in prehistoric times disetymologized and newly associated with the prefix *pri-*, cf. *prijьmьnъ, privǫzьnъ* (Czech *přátelstvo, přízeň*, cf. Machek 1957, 400), etc. Other explanations, e.g. importing from non-contraction area to the periphery, are also possible.

4. CONCLUSION

4.0 This stage is called the jer stage because the only condition for it is $A^1 = ь\ (ъ)$.

4.1 This means that it is a question of a phonetic process, i.e., regardless of the system. By the presence of Ā, however, this surface process penetrates even to the level of system, cf. 3.1. Of course, in the phonological system it could not achieve any fundamental changes, cf. 3.2.

4.2 In morphology, it affected chiefly the substantives, which in the course of this one phase made up for the headstart of other parts of speech besides the adjectival type *tretí*. Because almost the whole paradigm was subject to this change at the same time, this change means a fundamental incursion into the declension, not, however, through a disruption of equilibrium, but through a replacement of old relationships by new proportions.

In the system there already existed contraction paradigms; if these new proportions were created, then this not only was not a disruption of equilibrium, but, exactly to the contrary, it was the fulfillment of the intentions of the system.

4.3 But there are also cases that were contra-systemic, like the present *pěšь*. They were suppressed, in some languages, completely without exception (in Czech, however, we have forms like *zabím, zab,* which belong today to the type *prositi*), and frequently so thoroughly that their very existence came to be doubted, as in Slovak and Polish (cf. 1.4).

PART THREE

CONTRACTION
AS A NEW SYSTEMIC FACTOR

CHAPTER XII

GENERAL AND SPECIFIC FEATURES
OF CONTRACTION

1. GENERAL RULES, CONCEPTS, AND PHENOMENA

1.1   For contraction this rule is generally valid:

$$T^+A_1IA_2 \rightarrow T^+\bar{A} \qquad (12)$$

1.2   Here it is necessary particularly to stress

$$T^+ \rightarrow N \qquad (12')$$

which is an absolutely essential condition. Two phenomena attest
to the necessity of this condition:
   1.   The form *dobrěji* (Dat.Loc. sing. fem. adj.) is never
contracted, not even when there are the strongest internal stimuli
at hand (a whole contracted paradigm) and direct external stimuli (the forms *ký, mý, tý, pěší*, etc.). The reason is that the hard
paradigm requires hardness of the final stem consonant. But
since the form *dobrěji* has a soft consonant in this position, a
morphological change of the transformation would mean a change
$T' \rightarrow T^-$. This would be in conflict with (12), so that it could
not be realized. This means that even the strongest morphological stimuli cannot affect T^+. The change *dobrěji* > *dobrěj*, etc.,
is later and stems from the fact that contraction could not occur.
   If *dobrějemb* contracts to *dobrěmb* (c.f., e.g., Old Czech
dobrěm), then it is only as a result of phonological stimuli in
MF. The form *dobrěji* could not be contracted until MM; here
there were no phonological stimuli and thus it did not contract.
   2.   The form *moji* in the Nom. pl. masc. is the only form
of the plural in Czech that does not undergo contraction. Even
cases like the Gen. pl. *mojichъ* > *mýchъ*, etc., are contracted
and, of course, almost all forms of the singular (though on *mojb*
cf. XI/2.3 ff.), which in this case have almost consistently
parallel coalesced forms in the hard declension of adjectives of
the type *dobrý*. Even the Gen. pl. has it in the form *dobrýchъ*
and the Nom. pl. masc. has it in the form *dobří*, nevertheless,
the form *moji* does not contract.

The ExD. for this form has the ending -*i*, which assumes the softness (including the palatalization) of the preceding consonant in opposition to the morpheme -*ý*, which is in the Nom. sing. masc. If this indispensible morphological requirement, i.e., the presence of the variant 'ï, were applied to the contraction of the form *moji*, i.e., if it became *m'ï, then it would be in conflict with (12'), because this contraction is not realized despite strong internal and direct external stimuli. And this proves the general validity of this formula.

The fact that T is not subject to any influences of contraction, that it is excluded from any process of contraction, shows its independence of the following vowel. In a system of integrity of syllables (syllabic harmony is only one of its consequences), this is a further indication of the inorganic status of contraction in the old phonological system and of its destructive innovativeness.

1.3   The whole kernel of the process, i.e., the systemic epoch of contraction, falls into two parts: the part in which phonological laws operate and the part in which exclusively morphological factors operate. For the first part, $D < 1$ is valid, for the second, $D > 1$, in which, at the point of contact of the two rules, i.e., at $D = 1$, lies MF. This stage links the phonological and morphological factors, never universally, but in stages — with phonemic factors still dominant in the first phase of this stage but with morphological factors dominating in the second. For the first part of the period, i.e., until $D = 1$, the qualitative principle $\bar{A} = A^2$ (the principle of the regressivity of contraction) applies, while in the further stages, i.e., from $D = 2$ onward, the quality of the contract is governed by morphological considerations; however, the principle $\bar{A} = A^2$ is respected by the majority of cases and is carried out even in the typologically succeeding stage, i.e., in J.

2.   FURTHER FEATURES OF THE SYSTEMIC EPOCH OF CONTRACTION

2.1   The systemic factors of contraction can have positive properties, when they generate contraction, or negative properties, when they block contraction. As long as the process is unrealized because of these negative features, we call this a negative process. Both phonological and morphological factors can be negative.

2. The conflicts of the systems rest on the clash of the antagonistic interests of the phonological and morphological systems; we speak, therefore, of INTERSYSTEMIC CONFLICTS. Intrasystemic conflicts occur when elements of the old quality encounter elements of the new quality and the old principles encounter the new principles. Often the new principles from the phonological and morphological planes unite against the old principles. Thus, we speak of INTERSYSTEMIC COORDINATION.

2.3 The phonological conditions for the realization of MF and M were formulated by the requirement of proximity of the two contrahends, and that is either direct proximity — $D = 1$ — or indirect proximity — $D = 2$. Cf. VIII, XI, concerning MF and M.

2.4 The morphological conditions for the realization of M and MM were formulated by the requirement of facultative conditioning — sufficient for the realization of M — and obligatory conditioning — mandatory for the realization of MF. Cf. IX, X, concerning these two stages.

3. THE CHRONOLOGICAL RELATIONSHIP OF THE INDIVIDUAL STAGES

3.1 The consistent succession of the stages, expressed by the regular increase in the value of D, but especially the mutual coherence of the evidence, does not leave much room to doubt the chronology adduced.

3.2 There still remains one more fundamental question, whether this complex of individual stage is a DISCRETE PROCESS or a CONTINUOUS one. The relatively brief length of time with which one must reckon as a consequence of it argues for a continuity of process. This consideration is further supported by the observation of the continuity and colligation among the processes of the individual stages. Greater and greater modifications of fundamental principles create new stages, as though repeating anew the original leitmotif in newer, richer, and more profound variations. Empirical reasoning suffices to this point.

3.3 Further, more profound analysis affords us the following additional data:

I. Each stage contains elements of future stages in embryonic form. Thus, P is already molding the whole future process of

contraction: it is molding the basic elements of the process —
the contract with its characteristic contraction quantity — and
even forming the first contracting morphological system already
— the paradigm of adjectives in the indirect cases of the plural:
dobryjichъ, pěšijichъ > dobrýchъ, pěšíchъ[1], cf. VI. The reader
will himself be able to enumerate, in accordance with the preceding chapters, the embryonic elements in suceeding stages.

II.   On the other hand, at the beginning of a new stage the
processes of the preceding stage always fade. Here it is useful to
underline the concrete data of phasic and chronological interference which were obtained by analysis of the individual stages,
viz.,

1.   Phonetic motives, i.e., elements of process P, play a
fundamental role in the rise of F and MF cf. VII/2.1.2,
VIII/2.1.3.

2.   MF, (cf. VIII) as a whole is the stage in which the
transformation of phonetic and phonological motives into morphological motives is best perceived. This is particularly true with
reference to the coexistence and cooperation of the two systemic
levels. MF may be defined as the point of contact of the two
chronologically adjacent stages F and M, cf. XII/1.3. This
definition appositely gives a true picture of the continuity of the
contraction process.

3.   The morphological stages M and MM are also, of
course, heirs to earlier features: they are realized through contracts, i.e. phonologically, (and consequentially, also phonetically);
but what is more, they are compelled to govern themselves by
the further phonetic rule (12') even against their own intentions
(cases like *dobrěji, moji* > N, cf. XII/1.2). M, which is close
to MF, has one phonological requirement more, i.e., D = 2 (9),
cf. IX/1.1, whereas for MM the value of D is irrevelant, cf. X/1.0.

4.   In arguments, XI/2.4-5, it was also shown that J overlaps MM and obviously was in contact with M.

---

[1] This is an unintentional development, i.e. it does not have the future
of contraction as its purpose. The same completely morphologized, super-
ficially identical process in the non-contraction languages (East Slavic,
Bulgarian) well demonstrates its fully morphological function.

III. The fluidity and permeability of the stages, however, in the central region did not lead to the loss of their systemic autonomy and internal consistence. Each of the stages success-fully realizes its intention: F establishes the contract and con-traction length as new systemic facts; MF frees the fixed structure of the syllable, takes the first steps toward the softness correlation of consonants, and forms morphological prospects (cf. the be-ginning of the contraction of pronouns); M forms the contraction paradigms and MM completes them. The picture is different on the periphery, especially in South Slavic. In the South Slavic contraction area, which the whole process of contraction reached later, the stages formed helter-skelter and were not able to stabilize their categories properly. Thus, morphological con-siderations reach as far as F (*lajati* > N), and may prevent the phonological results (this concerns chiefly the new, contraction quantity) from being established. In South Slavic, as a matter of fact, it is, in this stage, a matter of morphonological develop-ment, which means that the next stage (West Slavic MF) is practically already realized as morphological with a most im-portant consequence: it will fail to enforce the new phonological quality, i.e., the destruction of the original structure of the syllable and the rise of the softness correlation. On part of the Slavic territory, the fall of the jers overlapped the entire pro-cess, with corresponding systemic consequences. As we can see, in the South Slavic area the helter-skelter process led to the destruction of the individual, especially the phonological, stages, so that the phonological results of contraction were here not carried out: either they had to subordinate themselves to the old system (quantity) or evidently not to occur at all (the soft-ness correlation). On the West Slavic periphery, on the contrary, the later, i.e., morphological, motivations probably weakened first, cf. Old Polish *działajesz*. The difference between the focus and the periphery could be expressed in the following manner:

D =	0	1	2	3
e.g.	*aja* > *á*	*oja* > *á*	*aje* > *á/é/ó*	*oji* > *ý*
Focus	FF	MF	M	MM
Periphery	MF	M	MM	

TABLE 8

The central area outside the focus would appear between these two extremes, i.e. its F would have D = 0-1, its MF's D = 1-2, etc.

If the boundaries of the individual stages are fluid, if the stages can overlap and even (in South Slavic) merge and reciprocally deform one another, a question arises concerning the sense of such a precise dissection as was carried out in the preceding chapters. Is it not too minute and unnatural to correspond to the true reality of things?

It does not correspond to reality to the extent that this is identified with the surface. If we had witnessed the process of contraction (whether as its contemporaries or at least as retrospective observers with solid historical material), its development would probably seem to us not to be according to the preceding chapters, but to be much more a process without boundaries, consequently like an amalgam and full of inconsistencies, as was brought out in 3.3. It is quite justified to claim that as the witnesses of this process we would have found the chapters VI-XI provide the closest possible systemic interpretation of this empiric "chaos".

It is otherwise in our case, when the surface information is not at our disposal, when we are working not with concrete, but with structural material, i.e., not with superficial phenomena, but in essence with systemic underlying elements and units. These lead us rather accurately — with the help of adequate, i.e., systemic, in-depth analyses — not to the formulation of "real", i.e., superficial development, but to the construction of the development in the underlying structure. This systemic analysis not only gives us exact information on systemic developments, but itself, *mutatis mutandis,* the basis for the construction of relevant processes of the "real", superficial level that are unattainable by other means. Whereas, in the "material" stages (modern or historical, but well attested), the surface comes first, in the "non-material" stages the primary task must be the construction of a systemic, deep level as the initial.

4. TRIPLE CONTRAHENDS

4.0   By triple contrahends we understand cases of the type

$$T^+ \quad A1IA2IA3 \qquad\qquad (12!)$$

which, because they have the possibility of two different realizations, merit special attention.

4.1 Expression (12!) can be understood as two different contraction clusters for which it is valid that:

    1. First Cluster: $A^1 = A^1/1$, $A^2 = A^2/1$

    2. Second Cluster: $A^2 = A^1/2$, $A^3 = A^2/2$

in which, in the contrahends with two indices, the second index designates the sequence of the cluster and the first index the sequence of the contrahend in the cluster.

4.2 The deciding factor for the developmental chronology of these clusters is their value D (for the formulation of this value, see (6) in VIII/1.2.2), which determines the stage in which the contracting cluster will contract: the lower the value, the earlier the stage, cf. (7), (8), (9), (10). Therefore, in the form *čъjejě*, for example, wherein the first cluster has a D value of 2, the second cluster with $D = 1$ will develop earlier. On the other hand, in the form *čъjejǫ*, with the first cluster $D = 2$ and with the second cluster $D > 2$, the first cluster will develop earlier. If the D values are indentical in both clusters, then priority of development rests in the internal relationships of the stage, which will be analyzed in concrete cases in 4.4.1., case 2: *čъjeji* and in 4.4.2, case 1: *mojejě*.

By this contraction, whether in the first cluster or the second, the number of contrahends is lowered to two, i.e., expression (12") assumes the form:

$$TĀ^1IA^2/TA^1IĀ^2 \qquad (12!')$$

which are only concrete realizations of the general contracting cluster in (12), cf. XII/1.1. That which is retrospectively, i.e., DIACHRONICALLY, understood as a CONTRACT, here, according to (12), enters into the next, just being realized, i.e., SYNCHRONIC, stage as a CONTRAHEND, so that it is valid that:

$$TĀ^1IA^2/TA^1IĀ^2 = TA^1IA^2 \qquad (12,4)$$

This formula expresses the well-known principle of qualitative irrelevance in a contracting cluster (cf. *ъ* : *i*, *ъ* : *y*; IV/3.1) with subsequent consequences, on which see further in 4.5.

4.3   We shall not consider cases of the type *bojuješъ*, where there are sufficient reasons for the negative process; nor shall we bring into consideration the forms *dobryjejě, dobrojejǫ*, for these are old cases which, for this period, we consider in the shorter forms *dobryjě, dobrǫjǫ/dobrojǫ*. In essence, this does not mean that the principle of the triple contrahend could not be applied to most uncoalesced forms, but some of our conclusions nevertheless indicate that it is in coalesced forms that they must originate, cf. XV/1.3.[1]

4.4   We are left then, obviously only with the oblique cases of the singular of the possesive pronouns *čí, mojъ,* and the adjectival type *treti,* specifically the Genitive, Dative/Locative, and Instrumental fem.

4.4.1   The pronoun *čí:*

I. Genitive *čъjejě* 1. First cluster: *ъje,* D $=2$
2. Second cluster: *ejě,* D $= 1$

which means that the second cluster, as the cluster with the lower value od D, will develop earlier; and so in MF *čъjejě > čъjě;* the D of this contracted form is greater than 2 and it develops into *čě* only in MM.

II. Dative *čъjeji* 1. First cluster: se above I., D $= 2$
2. Second cluster: *eji,* D $= 2$

According to the value of D, both clusters could contract simultaneously in M.

1. First cluster: *čъjeji* $>$ *čěji*
2. Second cluster: *čъjeji* $>$ *čъji*

There are no valid reasons why one of these possibilities should be given priroity. Conformity to the paradigm, wherein *čъje-* was originally the obligatory basis for the oblique cases, argues for the first possibility. But after the change in the Genittive — cf. the preceding paragraph — this obligatoriness was lost. The adduced change in the Genitive, which is In., for ExD. can

---

[1]   Although the thesis that the longer forms were involved in the contraction is emphasized by some scholars (recently Mareš 1970, 527), there is no dependable way of proving it. On the other hand, W. R. Schmalstieg 1971, 136, offers new proofs that only the shorter forms could exist. However, for the final outcome this problem is not of primary importance.

be the forms *pěší, naší*, etc., argues for the second possibility. But the second possibility leads to a combination of phonemes which is unknown to the system. Did the system avoid this by contracting the form according to the first possibility? Even here it is at the disposal of ExD. in the form *méji,* cf. 4.3.2, paragraph 2. We reckon, then, in this stage, with the doublet *čěji/čí,* which in MM merged into the single form *čí.*

III. *čьjejǫ* 1. First cluster: see above I., D = 2

2. Second cluster: *ejǫ,* D = 3

Here the first cluster develops first, i.e. *čьjejǫ* > *čějǫ,* and then in M, in the following stage, there arises *čǫ́.*

4.4.2 The pronoun *mojь* always has D = 1 in the first cluster, i.e., *oje;* in the second cluster, D is the same as it is in the same cases of the pronoun *čí,* i.e., in the Genitive D = 1, in the Dative and Locative D = 2, in the Instrumental D = 3.

I. *mojejě* 1. D = 1; 2. D = 1

Here the second cluster has priority; that is to say, we have here an MF which has broken down into two phases; the second cluster contracts in the first phase; the first cluster could contract only in the following phase. It is valid, then, that *mojejě* > *mojě,* which contracts in the following period into *mé.*

II. *mojeji* 1. D = 1; 2. D = 2

Here the first cluster has priority, in a similar manner as in *mojego* > *mégo,* etc., i.e., *mojeji* > *méji.* Further development will be discussed in 4.5.

III. *mojejǫ* 1. D =1; 2. D   2

This form develops as follows: *mojejǫ* > MF *méjǫ* > MM *mǫ́.*

4.5 Theoretically very interesting and instructive with regard to 4.2 is the development of the form *méji* from 4.4.2, case 2. According to XIII/3 and table 9, the phoneme *é* has the value |2, 3|; *i,* then, according to tables 6 and 6" VIII/1.2, has the values |1,1|; then

$$D = |2 - 1| + |3 - 1| = 3$$

so that development would have to be realized according to (10), consequently, in MM, X/1.0.

But the development of the contracting cluster *méji* is subject to formula (12.4) in XII/4.2, i.e. the quantity of *é* is here irrelevant, for *é* is here interpreted as a contrahend. It is not, consequently, related to that element of table 9, representing the system of contracts, but to that of tables 6 and 6", representing the system of contrahends. The element *é,* then, inarguably belongs in table 6 in the place of *e,* i.e., one place higher than in table 9, so that its value is [2, 2]; the decisive difference of the cluster discussed is, then:

$$D = |2 - 1| + |2 - 1| = 2$$

so that, according to (9), (IX/1.1), the development *méji* > *mý* was realized in M. This chronology is of substance for whereas M requires facultative morphological conditioning, MM would require obligatory conditioning, cf. IX/1.3, especially 1.3.3; and X/1.1. This conditioning remains weak: the forms *naší, pěší* are, no doubt, contracted, but the ExD. itself, the form *dobřěji,* remains uncontracted cf. XII/4.2, case 1, *passim* and is, therefore a negative factor for development. If there are in Old Czech the doublets *mý/méj* (< *méji*), then it is self-evident that in the development *méj* > *mý* there is lacking an explanation of *éj* > *ý.* On the other hand, the secondary rise of the form *méj* after *dobřěj, dobréj* is without problems, cf. Marvan 1964.

4.6   Next into consideration come the compound forms of the adjective *tretí.* Because we assume that the nominal forms of this adjective contracted only as a result of J, cf. Chapter XI, the contraction of compound adjectives of this type was realized in exactly the same way as in the type *pěší,* i.e., e.g., *tretьjaja* > *tretьjá* as *pěšaja* > *pěšá,* etc. In J, then, the development of the type *tretьjá* > *treťá* was achieved; A¹ could not in any way influence the agreement between the two adjectival types; the compound form of the adjectival type *tretí* (*boží* . . . etc.) integrated with the type *pěší.* Because the majority of nominal forms of this type also had similar forms, here the opposition between nominal and adjectival forms was lost. This loss had already begun, as a matter of fact, at the dawn of contraction, in P, wherein the nominal forms *tretьjь,* etc., and the compound forms *tretьjьjь,* etc. develop in the same way.

4.7   The assumption that the compound feminine adjective enters into contraction in an unreduced form (e.g., *dobry-jejě,* etc;

cf. 4.2) would make it possible to presume for this adjective contracting clusters of more than three contrahends, too. Thus, as the counterpart to the hypothetical forms *pěšě-jejě, pěši-jeji* with contracting clusters of three contrahends there would be the forms *tretь jě-jejě, tretьji-jeji* with four contrahends; to a form *pěšejǫ-jejǫ* with four contrahends would be contraposed a form *tretьjejǫ-jejǫ* with five contrahends. Forms of this type, however, we must consider as purely hypothetical and for our purposes, as was pointed out in 4.2, are excluded.

4.8 Coalescence in the imperfect does not belong to the process of contraction. Its outcome, however, i.e., a long coalesced vowel, is preserved as a contract in a system in which there is contraction. Therefore, forms of the type (*lajaachъ* >) *lajáchъ* develop as the second phase of triple contrahends, i.e., the contract enters into contraction. The contraction *lajáchъ* > *láchъ*, therefore, agrees with changes like *mojě́* > *mé*, etc.; it is, however, older: it is realized in the type *lajati* in F, in the type *grějati* in MF, in the type *prьjati*, of course, only in MM.

CHAPTER XIII

SIGNIFICANCE OF CONTRACTION FOR THE DEVELOPMENT OF THE PHONOLOGICAL SYSTEM

1. THE RISE OF THE NEW QUANTITY

1.0   The real outcome of contraction is the rise of an entirely new type of quantity.

1.1   This new phonological category enters into a system that already knows quantity. The new category enters into conflict with the old system.

1.2   An example of this onslaught is the treatment of such old quantitaive opposition as ь : i, e : ě as in a certain sense irrelevant, cf. *pěšьjь* > *pěší* : *pěšiji* > *pěší,* similarly, *pěšeje//pěščjě* > *pěšě.* Of course, the fact that in a contracting cluster even contracts are treated in the same manner points to a specific feature of this conflict — here there is an opposition not of two systems, but of the old system against the new CATEGORY of contract. Only in the center of the process of contraction, in the West Slavic languages — with certain reservations — did this category prevail over the old prosodic system, which had to adapt itself to it. In the remaining contraction territory, of course, it was not lost, but the relationship of forces was here reversed — the old system prevailed, the new category adapted itself to it.

1.3   It is, however, characteristic of the whole contraction territory that the old quantitative differences were preserved precisely in them and only in them, so that the conflict betwen the old system and the new category also had its positive side in the coordination and strengthening of the quantitative oppositions as a whole.

1.4   On the relationship of other old prosodic categories to the new categories in West Slavic, see XVIII/2.

1.5   The rise of the category of contract led, even though by stages, on the basis of the opposition A :Ā, to a revaluation of the old oppositions. If we follow the development closely, then we find at first the contract could assume only such qualitative forms as corresponded to the quality of vowels originally long, like *á, ú,* etc. The rise of *ó* is, for example, much later; in some languages perhaps it did not develop at all in the course of contraction. In connection with this the problem of I and *é* is especially instructive.

2. THE PROBLEM OF THE ELEMENT I

2.0 Because of requirements for the investigation of contraction there was introduced in IV the symbol $I = ь/i/ъ/y$ so that the expressions after the equals sign in a contraction are neutralized.

2.1 This formulation does not mean that we are dealing with the variants of a single phoneme. On the contrary, in the precontraction system we recognize all four elements as separate phonemes, cf. *gad ъ* : *gady, gadi* : *gady, šestъ* : *šestь, šestь* : *šesti.* We recognize further that at least quantitative distinctions also survived into the period of contraction, on which distinctions J, which results from the weakening of jers (cf. *pьješь* > *péšь,* but *šiješь* > N), is built.

2.2 Nevertheless, the oppositions among these four phonemes are irrelevant for the category of contract, which leads to the introduction of the construct Ī. This construct contains, therefore, four forms that are phonemes in the old system. The fact that the relationship Ī : I represents the same correlation as *á* : *a,* *ǫ́* : *ǫ* . . . (on the morphological consequences of this opposition see XIV/1) justifies this hypothesis synchronically. Further development, connected with the basic influence of contraction on the system, confirms this hypothesis diachronically: first, quality is lost as a distinctive feature, then the "jer phoneme" is lost (on the influence of contraction on the fall of the jers, see especially XVII/3). The construct I, then, becomes a real element of the phonological system.

3. THE PROBLEM OF THE ELEMENT *é*

3.0 This sound is conditioned by its position after T⁻; it is necessary, therefore, to understand it as a variant.

3.1 Usually, it is simply considered to be an automatic variant of the phoneme *e,* cf. Komárek 1962, 47, "the back *e*", likewise Pauliny 1963, 44. But this is impossible because *é* is excluded after T'. Every *e* in Ā is reflected as *ě́*, cf. VII.

3.2   If *e* is reflected in Ā as *ě́*, then that means that it is a variant not of *e*, but of *ě́*. The sounds *ě́/é* form, then, a single phoneme $^+$*ě́*, in the same manner as *'á/á* $=^+$ *a*, *í/ý* $=^+$*ī*, etc., so that, according to table 6 in VIII/1, the system of contrahends in West Slavic may be written as

	0	1	2	3	4	5
1		ī			ú	
2	('ḗ)					ǫ́
3			ě́	á		

TABLE 9

3.3   This phonological character of *é* is extraordinarily important for the chronology of the rise of West Slavic quantity. Since no other *é* stands in this opposition, but on the contrary, its position after T' precludes the possibility of opposition with *ě́* — cf., e.g., Old Czech *nesu* : *nésti, nesla* : *nésl, žeru,* but *žéřeš, sěmena* : *seménko,* etc. — it is obvious that the rise of *é* $=^-$*ě́* precedes the rise of *'é*, i.e., that contraction preceded the re-valuation of intonation into quantity, that, therefore, it was its precedent. This argumentation we shall use in XVII.

3.4   It is apropos here also to call attention to why, in contradistinction to ɪ, we do not overlook the opposition *e* : *ě* as irrelevant, despite what is said in 1.2. Contraction here, in contradistinction to oppositions with jers, not only does not weaken the correlation, but actually further strengthens it. The system has the pair *e* : *o* and the pair *o* : *a*, in which irrelevance in contraction is excluded. The same proportion exists in the pair *e* : *ě*. In both of the last two pairs only the second member is realized as a contract. The different relationships of the vowels *e, ě* to the whole system of vowels in the various stages of contraction are important. In both, the relationships of immediate and un-hampered proximity are realized according to table 9, which fixes their various positions in the system.

4. THE LOOSENING OF THE STRUCTURE OF THE SYLLABLE
AND THE RISE OF THE CATEGORY OF THE SOFTNESS CORRELATION
OF CONSONANTS

4.0 Until the rise of contraction, the principle of syllabic harmony was valid, cf. IV/4, which was realized thus:

T^+	$a,\ u,\ \varrho$
T^-	$o,\ y,\ ъ$
T'	$e,\ ě,\ ę,\ i,\ ь$

TABLE 10

These proportions not only were valid, but were also established everywhere where there might be resistance to this system, cf. (4.4!) in IV/4.1.

4.1 The development (12') $T^- \rightarrow$ N in contraction means that syllables break these bonds first.

4.2 This rule would operate wholly without consequences if the qualitative relationship $\bar{A} = A^1$ were valid, for the proportion $T^+ A^1$, inherited from the system represented by table 10, would have been preserved. However, already in the initial phase of contraction, in P, according to (6), VI/2.2, there appears a second development possibility in which the quality of the contract is determined by A^2. For West Slavic, the conception of contraction as a unitary process makes this interpretation possible, for in all stages of contraction in which the differences between A^1 and A^2 can be manifested in $\bar{A}$, where $A^1 = A^2$, i.e., beginning from MF, and where, of course, there are no morphological motives standing in the way, the qualitative principle $A = A^2$ is actually carried out.

4.3 In a situation in which $\bar{A} = A^2$, a breakdown of the system occurs. T^+ here develops quite evidently absolutely independently of $\bar{A}$, so that in the contracts the pairs of variants $\bar{A}/'\bar{A}$ begin to be formed, cf. table 9. If these pairs represent variants of a single phoneme, then the pair T^-/T' must represent two phonemes which differ in softness. Thus arises the category of the softness correlation of consonants.

Thus, for example, Komárek 1962, 46: "The consonant that preceded a vowel that had arisen through coalescence was soft if the vowel had arisen through the contraction of a cluster with a front vowel as its initial vowel . . . This fact has great importance for the development of the paired softness of consonants". However, the claim at the conclusion of the book, on p. 177: "Neither through coalescence nor through the vocalization of jers do new phonemes arise" considerably contradicts this statement.

4.4 We call this phenomenon a category not because it is a question of a new opposition: a closely related opposition did exist, however, it was limited only to plosive sonorants, viz., $l : \hat{l}$ ($< lj$), $r : \acute{r}$ ($< rj$), $n : \acute{n}$ ($< nj$), cf. I/1 and also the opposition $\varnothing : I$. This opposition non-palatal : palatal (!) does not constitute a category (cf. the new Czech opposition $d : d'$, $t : t'$, $n : \check{n}$). The contraction, on the other hand, generates an opposition hard : soft (i.e., palatalized, where the palatalization is originally positional, i.e. allophonic) which covers most of the consonants, i.e., $l : l'$, $r : r'$, $n : n'$; $b : b'$, $p : p'$, $m : m'$, $w : w'$; $d : d'$, $t : t'$; $z : z'$, $s : s'$ (11 pairs), so that for well-known reasons only the series $g : d\check{z} : d\acute{z}$; $k : \check{c} : \acute{c}$ and $x : \check{s}$ were passed over.

4.5 It seems to be essential to investigate this process in somewhat greater detail. On the surface, i.e., at the empirical level, it is as though nothing, or almost nothing, had occurred. Before the vowel i (likewise before $\acute{i}$) there always occur the consonants l'. . . b'. . . d'. . . z'. . . etc., whereas before the vowel $y/\acute{y}$ there always occur their hard counterparts. Not even such new combinations as $d'a$, $d'u$, etc. empirically contradict the rules of harmony; on the contrary, these combinations further extend the validity of the rules. In the underlying system, however, almost everything was changed. Harmony loses its vitality because the rule of syllabic harmony (cf. IV/4, especially formulae (4.4a) and (4.4!)) disappears and is replaced by rule (12) in XII/1. Syllabic harmony in its classical form is limited to non-contracting syllables; it begins to be unproductive, until it is lost completely. If we wished to call the new state syllabic harmony, then it would be typologically an entirely new system. Whereas in the original, Proto-Slavic system, both consonantal and vocalic phonemes were deciding factors, and always in the direction of the marked form, in this system only consonants are deciding factors, but in both directions. It would be possible to compare this new stage with the relationships in modern Polish or Russian, where one cannot speak of syllabic harmony, cf. XIII/4.10.

4.6 The disintegration of the contraction territory in the period when this category of the palatalization correlation has to dominate is striking; South Slavic territory resisted this radical systemic interference. The later analogical process in J had already ceased to enforce this principle.

4.7 The retreat of epenthetic *l* is obviously connected with the rise of this category as a consequence of contraction, and this precisely in West Slavic, at least in final syllables. The earlier forms *bl', pl', ml', wl'* (on whose rise and nature cf. I), which expressed the softness of the labials *b, p, m, w* on the surface, cf. *zeml'a* : *voňa*, lost their right of surface existence through the rise of the phonemes *b', p', m' w'* and were replaced by these phonemes. By this the underlying units *b', p', m', w'* gained adequate counterparts on the surface as well.

4.8 The fact that ONLY West Slavic, which does not change *x* to *š* in the second palatalization develops the opposition *s* : *s'*, might be of considerable importance. If it is true that palatalization did not extend to the position *s'*, because this position had already been filled, this can have substantial significance in the revision of the chronology and course of palatalization. Because contraction is indisputably more recent than palatalization but the formation of the series *x* : *š* : *s* might be still more recent, this series would arise much later than palatalization through mere imitation of the model *g/k* : *dž/č* : *dź/ć*. Then, of course, in the case of *x*, it is not a question of palatalization at all, but of a process with which Meillet reckoned, i.e. that the chronologically oldest member of the triad *x* : *š* : *s* was not *x*, but *š;* further members were formed according to the model cited; in the period when the matter had to be resolved by the formation of the third member *s*, in the West Slavic languages the position was already occupied and *š* could not change. This concept of Meillet's, as is well-known, has important consequences for the determination of Balto-Slavic relationships.

4.9 The rise of the category of the palatalization of consonants is closely connected with the existence of contrahends: the category is realized ONLY in the position before a contrahend. This is a further important corroboration of the hypothesis of the exceptionality of the modern category of the contract in the old phonological system. Both of the new categories are closely interrelated; in a syllable with a contract there obtain entirely different relationships from those in the remaining syllables.

4.10   The circumstances that contraction has no influence on T^+ means that on West Slavic territory there is a large breach in the Proto-Slavic phonological system. Syllabic harmony as a phonological phenomenon retreats. The requirements of the marked harmonization of the syllable — if a consonant is soft, a following back vowel has to assimilate itself to it; but if a vowel is front, then a preceding hard consonant has to assimilate itself to it — are disregarded by contraction syllables. In these syllables there is always a deciding factor T^+ that influences the phonetic shape of the following $\bar{A}$. In a syllable T' A(f), $\bar{A}$(f) is only a variant of a phoneme, that in $T^-\bar{A}$ has the shape $\bar{A}$(b). The opposition $\bar{A}$(b) : $\bar{A}$(f)[1] is, consequently, phonetic and is phonologically irrelevant, whereas the opposition T^- : T' is phonological. These relationships can well be compared to, for example, modern Russian or Polish; e,g,, in Russian, in the opposition *sy* : *si, sa* : *s'a*, the pairs $|y|:|i|,|a|:|'a|$ represent phonetic, phonologically irrelevant opposition, whereas $|s|:|s'|$ is phonologically relevant opposition (and it is obviously not a question of syllabic harmony). The phonetic, superficial resemblance of the Proto-Slavic syllable and the contracting syllable — cf., e.g., Proto-Slavic *sy* : *si*, contracting *sý* : *sí, sá* : *s'á* — must not lead us to the identification of the two systems. In a contracting syllable, therefore, the strict structure of the Proto-Slavic syllable was loosened, there arose the softness correlation of consonants as a basic binary principle, and the opposition *ý* : *i* was dephonologized.

---

[1] A(b), A(f) symbolize here 'back/front A' respectively.

CHAPTER XIV

THE SIGNIFICANCE OF CONTRACTION FOR THE DEVELOPMENT OF THE MORPHOLOGICAL SYSTEM

1. CONTRACTION AND THE MORPHOLOGICAL SYSTEM

1. The systemic consequences of contraction in morphology, which will be the subject of this chapter, are connected with the basic feature of contraction, the rise of the contract.

1. The designation of the contract as a new PHONOLOGICAL category, cf. XIII, can also be applied to the morphological system. We shall, therefore, operate with the concept of the MORPHOLOGICAL category of the CONTRACT.

1.2 A consequence of contraction, which as is known, is also a process with morphological factors, is the creation of special paradigms in the adjective, pronoun, substantive, and verb, for which the contract as a morphological distinctive feature is characteristic.

1.3 Paradigms with this distinctive feature we shall call contraction paradigms; paradigms standing in opposition to the contraction paradigms we shall call non-contraction paradigms.

1.4. In the following paragraph we shall investigate this category in individual parts of spech. Because we are concerned with a systemic category we shall not, of course, take into consideration individual forms, isolated in the paradigm, with contracts like *gostě, gostí* . . . , *ženǫ́* . . . , *trě̃* . . . , and likewise contrasystemically arisen forms like *p'ǫ́, pěšь* . . . , *pí, krý* . . . , *zm'á* . . . will not be the subject of our investigation.

2. THE SUBSTANTIVE

2.0 After the exclusion of the individual, non-systemic cases in 1.4, there remain for analysis the cases that in historical grammars are traditionally referred to as *ijo/ija*- stems, i.e., the Proto-Slavic types *ulьjь, sǫdьja, lanьji, ostrьje*.

2.1 As is known, contraction in these paradigms as a whole arose at the very end of the process, when it seems that the process has already exhausted all its possibilities, when it seems that the substantive will remain aloof from the whole of this vast process that is encroaching deep into even the system of morphology, creating in other word types the new, contraction paradigms.

2.2 The unarguable fact that in J it is a matter of a phonetic process does not entirely exclude any systemic influence. Of course, these systemic influences have an entirely new character. The role of the phonological plane is assured by the chronological simultaneity of MM and J. The influence of the morphological plane compared with earlier stages, when it was a question of close contracts between contracted and uncontracted forms like ExD., had a much more integral character. In the period of J the contract exists as a morphological category, and the remaining flexible word types create contraction paradigms; the tendency of morphology toward the creation of this category even in substantives is evident.

2.3 The principle of the whole category and of the opposition of contraction and non-contraction paradigms is very simple in the substantives. The contraction paradigm is always soft and stands in complete opposition to the soft paradigm without a contract. which is, in this case, therefore, the non-contraction paradigm:

$$
\begin{array}{rcl}
krajь & : & úlí \\
sǫdьca & : & sǫd'á \\
bogyni & : & laní \\
more & : & ostr\acute{e} \\
\end{array}
$$
etc.

2.4 By complete opposition we understand the fact that the morphological category of contract is here symmetrically realized as the phonological category of contract, i.e., that a contrahend in an ending of a contraction paradigm stands to the corresponding vowel of the corresponding ending in the same relationship as the contrahend to a vowel of the same quality, that, therefore, in both planes the isomorphic relationship $\bar{A} : A$ is valid; therefore, for example, $á : a = úl'á : kraja, sǫd'á : sodьca$, etc., $í : ь/i = úlí : krajь, kraji; laní : bogyni$, etc.; also, of course, $úlimь : krajьmь, úlíchъ : krajichъ$, etc. Deviations from this principle, like Instrumental $lan'ǫ́ : bogyn'ǫ́$ (cf. Accusative $lan'ǫ́ : bogyn'ǫ$), we explain as quantitative neutralization.

2.5 This total equilibrium does not long survive and is already doomed to destruction at its very inception, for a process involved in its rise, the fall of the jers, contravenes it. Thus, there arise oppositions like *í* : *ø*, cf. *úlí* : *kraj; í* : *e*, cf. *úlím'* : *krajem'*, etc. In this period of the relaxing of strict equilibrium there also arise further possibilities for the disintegration of both types; the contraction paradigm achieves contact with the compound adjective, first in the plural. But this is already the period in which some territorial disintegration has occurred.

2.6 Slovak has preserved and even emphasized a relatively archaic form (cf., e.g., *list'ú* > *listiu* after *listie, listia,* in spite of the non-existence of a diphthong *iu*). Czech, in which the old opposition is recalled only to a very minor extent, has gone the farthest in differentiation. On the other hand, in the remaining contraction languages these oppositions were completely suppressed, in the Lechitic languages in connection with the loss of quantity, in South Slavic because the category of contraction did not prevail, but adapted to the original system.

3. ADJECTIVES

3.0 Contraction is the consummate autonomization of the compound adjective; through contraction is lost the compoundness of this declension (if it is still so called even in modern grammars, then this is a term of a new order, no longer descriptive but prescriptive) the new, adjectival declension is formed. This declension is the contraction paradigm.

3.1 It would be erroneous to assume automatically that the nominal forms of the adjective are the corresponding non-contraction paradigm. They belong, in fact, to the category of substantive and within its framework they can develop into opposition (cf. XIV/2; the oppositions concerned are *pĕšь, pĕša* . . . *tretí, tre-t'á* . . . , which differ in no way from substantival oppositions). The real reason for the incomparability of the nominal and the adjectival declension is that a number of endings have an entirely different structure, cf. *dobra* : *dobrégo/dobrógo, dobrъ* : *do-brýchъ,* etc.

3.2 On the other hand, the pronouns have the structure of their endings agreeing with that of the endings of the adjectival declension. Particularly easy to compare is the soft declension, cf. *pěší* : *našь*, *pěšégo* : *našego* . . . *pěšíchъ* : *našichъ* and, of course, the oblique cases of the sing. fem., like Genitive *pěšě* : *našě* (Sout Slavic *pěšę́* : *našę́*), cf. the following section. We find ourselves in an entirely different siuation in the hard declension, where there is, for example, *dobrégo*/*dobrógo* : *togo,* where only the periphery shows agreement, *dobrýchъ* : *těchъ,* etc. This relationship is, of course, not random; it reflects exactly the co-existence of two systems, in which the non-contraction paradigm reflects the old system and the contraction paradigm reflects the modern system. In the old system, *o* in the hard declension corresponds to *e* in the soft declension (*togo* : *našego, město* : *more,* etc.), *ě* corresponds to *i* (*ženě̌* : *duši*); in the new system the oppositions *é* : *č́, í* : *ý* are in agreement with the modern category of softness correlation. It is true that even in this case there remain certain irregularities, like *dobrémь* : *tomь, dobrěji* : *tý;* but these exceptional cases balance out, either within the paradigm itself, as *dobřém dobrém,* or by mutual integration, as *dobrěji*/ *dobréj*/*tý* → *dobréj*/*dobrý*//*tý*/*téj,* which attests to a real correlation.

3. In the adjective declension it is necessary in this period to abandon the notion of compoundness, which we shall then find represents the contraction paradigm of prononuns, adhering to the analogous proportion in relation to non-contraction paradigms as is the case with substantives. Even a number of real pronouns belong to this contraction paradigm, cf. *kъterý, taký, kaký, jaký;* in the process of contraction are formed *ký, čí,* partially also *mojь;* especially instructive are oppositions like *kégo* : *kogo, čégo* : *čego,* where the contract is the single distinctive feature of contraction forms as a whole, not merely of the endings.

3.4 Not only the relationships between contraction and non-contraction paradigms, but also the intersystem relationships among the contraction paradigms themselves are characteristic of the category of contract. Already prehistorically the contraction paradigm of definite adjectives begins strongly to influence the contraction system of substantives, cf. the Instrumental forms *kopím, kopími.* This process, thanks to specific favorable conditions, lasts, as a matter of fact, to this day, e.g., in Czech (cf. the substandard forms *zelího, zelímu* . . . , *paních* . . .).

4. PRONOUNS

4. The basic interparadigmatic opposition was determined by the fact that the adjectival declension (including cases as *ký, čí*) was characterized as the contraction paradigm of pronouns. But beyond this interparadigmatic opposition, within the non-contraction paradigms there exists in the pronoun an intraparadigmatic opposition.

4.1 The contraction system of intraparadigmatic opposition has a precise categorial delimitation. It is valid only for gender pronouns and only, of course, for those which themselves do not belong to a contraction paradigm, cf. 3.3.

4.2 This intraparadigmatic opposition can be formulated as a miniature counterpart of interparadigmatic opposition. Contraction and non-contraction forms have the same shapes; however, as though it were a matter of interparadigmatic differences, both these forms are united into a single, contractionally mixed paradigm.

4.3 Outwardly, however, this paradigm with internal opposition looks like a non-contraction paradigm, i.e., a paradigm standing in opposition to a contraction paradigm, which in the pronoun is represented by the adjectival declension. Such oppositions as *dobré : té . . . , pěší : naší* represent the same proportion as *pan'ǫ́ : bogyn'ǫ́,* which was explained in 2.4 as quantitative neutralization.

4.4 The fact that the non-gender pronouns remain apart from these oppositions is not surprising. Substantives of the hard paradigms also do not enter into these relationships, i.e., beyond the opposition, contraction paradigm : non-contraction paradigm, stands yet a further paradigm which does not have a systemically relevant contrahend.

4.5 In the focus there arises yet a third type of opposition that realizes the possibilities of both oppositions and both paradigms, i.e., the possibilities of contraction and non-contraction paradigms with the possibilities of intraparadigmatic oppositions. We are here concerned with the possesives *mojь, tvojь, svojь.* As a contraction paradigm this type has a shape corresponding to that of the hard adjectival declension (the forms *mojь* and Nominative plural masculine *moji,* whose non-contraction is diachronically motivated by the specifics of contraction, can, con-siding their exceptionality, be ignored in the same manner as the form *dobrěji* in the adjectival declension). As a non-contraction paradigm exhibits intraparadigmatic opposition, contraction forms are then limited to indirect cases (they always have the shape of the hard declension), whereas in the direct cases they correspond to the soft non-contraction soft declension (!) cf. *moja : naša, mojǫ : našǫ,* etc. In Slovenian in these pronouns we have a declension with intraparadigmatic opposition; here, of course, in contradistinction to the main opposition of contraction singular : non-contraction plural with a potential opposition in the singular similar to the Czech opposition, i.e., contraction indirect cases : non-contraction direct cases. The peripheral languages here have the same relationship as in the remaining gender pronoun.

5. CONJUGATION

5.0 Here we shall investigate both interparadigmatic oppositions that are realized in the present cf. *laješь : dělášь,* and intraparadigmatic oppositions that are realized in the preterite, cf. *dělachъ : děláchъ.*

5.1.0 The paradigmatic opposition of the contracting conjugation and the non-contracting conjugation arises in the so-called *j*-stem verbs; the remaining verbs do not enter into this opposition.

5.1.1 As *j*-stem verbs — and that purely as a label — we designate those verbs in which the formal part of the present stem exhibits the combination of a vowel with *j,* i.e., Segment I. The present stem of these verbs has, therefore, the shape

$$(TA)nI \qquad (14)$$

where *n* expresses the number of syllables in the stem. The combination of the stem vowel and *j* together with the following vowel of the ending forms a contraction cluster.

5.1.2 *J*-stem verbs can be divided according to the value of *n* into two classes:

1. Root verbs : n = 1
2. Suffixed verbs : n > 1

Root verbs are, therefore, the verbs *laješь, spěješь, čuješь, šiješь* . . . , suffixed verbs are *dělaješь, uměješь, kurpuješь* . . .

5.2 For the contraction of *j*-stem verbs in the present the following rules are valid:

1. Only suffixed verbs contract, i.e., a root vowel is not capable of contraction.

2. Only those verbs contract whose infinitive stem differs from the present stem, only in the absence of I $= j$, while the structure of (TA)^n must be the same, e.g. *děla/ti* : *děla/ješь* as opposed to the type *kupov/ati* : *kupuješь* which does not contract.

3. Only those forms contract for whose contracting cluster it is valid that A$^2 = e$ (the forms *dělajǫ, dělajǫtъ* . . . do not contract).

5.3 The category of contract in conjugation has several specific features:

1. In contradistinction to the pronouns, in which the bearer of the intraparadigmatic opposition was the non-contraction paradigm, here the bearer of this opposition is the contraction paradigm, cf. *děláš* : *dělajǫ*. Interparadigmatic opposition is realized according to rule 1, intraparadigmatic opposition according to rule 3 in 5.2.

2. The contrahend, i.e., the vowel, does not stand in opposition to the contract, rather the contracting cluster does, i.e., A : A^{1}IA^2, where A$^2 = e$, in which, for the quality of the contract, it is valid that A $=$ A^1, since A^1 is morphologically distinctive.

5.4 The consequences of these changes are:

1. Loss of many types of suffixed verbs.

2. Isolation of the type *kupuješь* and its later integration with root verbs into a single class.

3. Development of the contraction conjugation with great power of attraction.

3a. On the basis of these oppositions *děláš* : *laješь, uměš* : *spěješь* the opposition *prosišь* : *šiješь* was gradually formed.

3b. After the fall of the jers, when the number of syllables had become irrelevant, the contraction conjugation comes into contact with the so-called athematic verbs, still during the prehistorical period profoundly influences their endings, and in the historical period brings the contract even to the 1st person singular according to their model.

4. These changes strengthen the position of the present stem as the initial criterion for classification into a conjugation.

5.5 The intraparadigmatic opposition (Aor.) *dĕlachъ* : (Imperf.) *dĕláchъ* has several diachronic and synchronic peculiarities:

1. Diachronically, it is not a question of contraction, which would motivate the rise of this opposition, for contrahends were treated as the result of contraction in the imperfect only later. Then, however, they function as the category of contract.

2. Opposition refers to those cases in the first series in which both tenses are formed from the same base; the pairs *kryjĕchъ* : *krychъ*, *tisknĕchъ* : *tiščechъ*, etc. are not comparable.

3. The forms of the asigmatic aorist are forms that do not enter into opposition at all. Their successors, however, the forms *nesechъ* . . . are motivated by the imperfect *nesĕchъ*, which forms the appropriate opposition (the reasons why here we reconstruct *ĕ* instead of the traditionally reconstructed *á* are based on the attested forms in the contraction territory, cited in II/3.2.2).

4. In equilibrating the proportion between the contraction and the non-contraction systems, the following steps were taken:

4a. Modern, sigmatic forms, standing in complete opposition to the imperfect, cf. 3, were strengthened at the expense of the asigmatic aorist.

4b. Precisely on West Slavic territory we observe an express tendency toward the levelling of the endings of both systems.

4c. On this territory the imperfect of the type *prošáchъ* is also subject to adaptation.

5. Whereas interparadigmatic opposition concerns the whole contraction territory, this intraparadigmatic opposition clearly affects only West Slavic territory with the contiguous Slovenian.

5.6 Most characteristic of this internal opposition are two features: first, that it appears as an opposition outwardly too, i.e., that contraction and non-contraction forms do not vary freely, but stand in paired opposition; second, that there is a preponderance of cases in which the opposition Ā : A is the one distinctive feature not only of the formal part, but also of the words as a whole, cf. *dĕláchъ* : *dĕlachъ*, *vidĕchъ* : *vidĕchъ*, etc. At the same time, opposition of the type *láchъ* : *láchъ*, which, on the surface, looks like an identity, is systemically appropriate; here, too, as in substantives and pronouns, the neutralization of quantity is valid in the non-contraction system. The superficial identity, of course, forces subsequent differentiation.

6. GENERAL FEATURES OF THE MORPHOLOGICAL CATEGORY OF CONTRACT

6.0   The contract is not only the bearer of a new phonological category, but also of a new morphological category. Morphological systems, i.e., the paradigms or subordinate formations that are characterized by contraction systems, enter into correlation, with other morphological systems — non contraction systems — and that in the framework of a different word-type inflection; the adjectival declension, in this case, we define as the contraction paradigm of pronouns.

6.1   If we are concerned with opposition between whole paradigms, we call it interparadigmatic opposition; if we are concerned with opposition within a paradigm, we call it intraparadigmatic opposition. A paradigm with intraparadigmatic opposition can enter into an interparadigmatic opposition as its non-contraction member (in pronouns) or as its contraction member (in verbs).

6.2   The principle of basic symmetry, i.e., the agreement of the structure of endings in correlative paradigms, is valid for interparadigmatic opposition.

6.3   For a paradigm with internal opposition the following relationships are valid in interparadigmatic opposition:

dobrá   : *ta*   // *dobré* : *té*
děláš̆ъ   : *laješ̆ъ* // *dělajǫ* : *lajǫ*
děláchъ : *dělachъ* // *láchъ* : *láchъ*

i.e., beside forms standing in opposition there exist surface forms standing in formal agreement, which was interpreted as neutralization.

6.4   Is the substantive excluded from these relationships? It would be possible so to deduce from the relatively late establishment of contraction oppositions in this type. But intra-paradigmatic oppositions exist even here, even considering that its motivation is not purely morphological (more exactly, word-forming), but simultaneously word-forming and lexical, e.g.,

sǫdьji, kъněžá : sǫdьca // bratrъ, kъnędzь dědъ, otьcь.

listě,   vrbě . . . : more   // listъ, vrba . . . dědъ, žena . . . ;

this situation depends upon the archaic non-differentiation of these systems, cf. Marvan et al. 1963, 106.

6.5 For interparadigmatic opposition the relationship, which we designate as Q : Q', where Q designates a non-con-traction paradigm and Q' designates a contraction paradigm, is valid; paradigms that do not enter into this correlation we term P. The individual word-type systems have, then, the following representation:

Substantive:	non-soft P	soft Q	"iio/iia" Q'
Pronoun:	non-gender P	gender Q	compound Q'
Verb:	non j-stem P	root Q	suffix Q'

TABLE 11

In this table we try to retain the traditional terms, with the the knowledge, however, that in the new situation after con-traction they are only prescriptive (this concerns mainly the contraction system). In this case, it is chiefly a matter of making clear the diachronic relationships that bind the contraction sys-tem together. By non-soft substantive we mean all paradigms except the so-called jo/ja-stems, i.e., even the types *kostь, ka-my/kamenь, etc.*

6.6 Intraparadigmatic opposition, in regard to interpara-digmatic opposition, is realized in a special form when Q/Q' is concerned, and that either without reference to another paradigm, or in a transposed form when all paradigms in a correlative form are concerned:

Intraparadigmatic opposition type	word type	paradigm	examples
direct	Pronoun	Q	*ta, tǫ : té, tǫ́*
direct	Verb, pres.	Q'	*dĕlajǫ : dĕláş̌ь*
transposed	Substantive	P/Q : Q'	*listъ, kъnedzь : listé, kъnežá*
transposed	Verb, pret.	P/Q' : Q	*nesĕchъ, dĕláchъ : láchъ*

TABLE 11'

6.7 If we ask what the diachronic justification for these two types of intraparadigmatic opposition is, we find that only direct opposition arose on the basis of contraction, whereas transposed opposition arose from other motives. Both types agree in principle, but differ in detail.

6.8 The morphological category of contract has the following distinctive features:

1. Ā : A e.g., *dobrá : ta, dĕláchъ : dĕlachъ, ostrĕ́ : more,* which is the case when the morphological proportion corresponds to the phonological proportion; this example is also basic for morphology.

2. Ā : Ā, e.g., *dobré : té,* (Aor.) *láchъ :* (Imperf.) *láchъ, lan'ǫ́ : bogyn'ǫ́,* which are cases of neutralization.

3. Ā ∼ A, e.g., *dobrýchъ : tĕchъ* (cf. *pĕšíchъ : jichъ*), where the opposition preserves the new opposition : old opposition system.

4. Ā : A1IA2, e.g. *dĕláş̌ь : laješь, má : moja, dobrí : moji, tý : dobrĕji,* where the opposition expresses the correlation new phonological system : old phonological system.

The imperfect forms *láchъ : lajáchъ* we do not consider as an opposition, for here we would have to assume in the second form a combining of the old phonological systems with the modern fact of neutralization of the quantity of the contrahend. Moreover, the system cannot confirm we are dealing with a problem of quantitative neutralization, i.e., there does not exist a form which distinguishes instead of neutralizating.

The category of morphological contract as a distinctive morphological feature can also preserve in itself further features of the modern system: the modern phonological features of quantity (1., 2.), the modern softness correlation with its morphological consequences (3.), and the ability to contract (4.).

CHAPTER XV

SPECIAL RECONSTRUCTION IN DECLENSION

1. THE QUESTION OF CONTRACTION IN THE FORMS *tojǫ, ženojǫ*

1.0 Particular importance attaches to this question because here a negative process links Central Slovak with certain peripheral South Slavic dialects. In Central Slovak then, an entirely different chronology is assumed from that assumed for the other West Slavic languages.

1.1 However, the northern part of the South Slavic territory, i.e., Slovenian, Kajkavian, and Northern Čakavian develops in this direction exactly as the West Slavic languages, cf. Ramovš 1952, 58 *passim*. In regard to the fact that still other striking features, such as the development *oje* > *é* (partially in cases of the type *mojego* > *mégo*), from which further depends the rise of the forms *dobrégo, dobrému,* link this area with West Slavic territory, we consider this territory as a component of the central region, cf. III, especially diagram 1. The absence of the same features in Central Slovak relegates this dialect to the region of the South Slavic periphery, of which this feature is likewise characteristic. The explanation of Central Slovak South Slavicisms as merely a result of contact with South Slavic territory is not sufficient, cf. Pauliny 1963, 37.

1.2.0 In Old Czech and Old Polish the Instrumental singular of the pronoun *ta* reflects the form *tý*. But at variance with the corresponding Old Czech paradigmatic form *tú* stands the uncontracted form *toji* (< *toju* < *tojǫ*), but only in the adverbialized expression *mezi toji,* New Czech *mezitím* "meanwhile".

On this longer form cf. Vážný 1962, 134 where it is presumed, together with Gebauer 1958, 445, that the two forms *toju/tú* fall together into *tojú.* But here it is precisely the problem that this uncoalesced form stood outside the paradigm, so that influence by the paradigm is hardly possible.

Just as in the other cases, it is necessary to look for the irregularities of development that lead to such doublets as *tojǫ/tý* in differences in the function of the various systems. A morphologically unconditioned form is an extraparadigmatic form that has lost contact with the paradigm as a result of the adverbialization of the construction in which it functions. It, then, could contract only with the aid of phonological factors. Because this form did not contract, the cluster *ojǫ* was beyond the range of phonological factors and could contract only with the aid of morphological ones. This was realized in paradigmatic forms like *tojǫ, ženojǫ* and also *mъnojǫ,* etc.

1.2.1 This interpretation is not new; Trávníček 1935, 66f, stresses it. The fact that such a significant detail as *mezi toji* is otherwice disregarded is inexplicable and hardly reasonable from a methodological point of view. After all, we are not dealing with a whole, but with a definite body of facts, in which each detail can have an important systemic value.

1.3 This entire argument leads to the conclusion that the change *ojǫ > ǫ́ is* not phonological, but morphological, to which D = 2 quite clearly attests. It does not have much to say about the development of contraction itself as a whole, for the fact that in a definite territory this change was not realized says nothing about phonological relationships, but merely morphological relationships on the southern periphery. If there were here no morphological motives of the type (*dobrǫjǫ >*) *dobrǫ́,* as is known from other contraction languages, then this can only mean that there was no form *dobrǫ́* that might have arisen in F and that therefore, on this territory one must allow for an original form *dobrojǫ,* which, of course, could not contract. These are the basic points of the argument that causes us so many chronological problems. By establishing the chronology of 1) contraction, 2) the fall of jers for the whole contraction territory, cf. XVI/1, specifically 1.4, we shall have eliminated any doubts whatever about the character of the contraction *ojǫ > ǫ́.*

2. THE DEVELOPMENT OF THE FORMS *toji, dobřeji, mojeji,* DAT./LOG. SING. FEM.

2.0 The Old Czech form *tej/téj* is traditionally derived from *toi̯ < toji* with assimilation of *o* to *i̯,* cf. Trávníček 1935, 356, Vážný 1962, 133f. In Czech nothing is known of such an assimilation, if we rely on Gebauer's omniscient observation, cf. Gebauer 1962, 230 ff. It will not be, perhaps, far from the truth to state that this notion of regressive assimilation is a residue of the thesis of the *přehláska* (umlaut) *aj* > *ej*, which Trávníček 1935, 76 still upholds, but which nowadays has been abandoned, cf. Komárek 1962, 156.

The thesis has been abandoned, but the explanation of the form *tej/téj* by assimilation — for lack of another — has survived. Klemensiewicz et al. 1964 presume for Polish that this form is result of the influences of the soft pronominal declension, like *naszej, mojej,* cf. p. 315; but this cannot be applied to Czech for two reasons: on the one hand, *eji* is reflected in Czech as the contract *í,* cf. *naší, jí* — which, in no Polish dialect was wholly obligatory — on the other hand, the influence of the soft declension on the hard declension is not valid for Czech.

2.1   Contrary to this, the development *toji* > *tý* can be fully accepted as MM. The form *tý,* which, without an analysis of the contraction, confuses considerably and leads to such diachronisms as the explanation (*ý* > *ej* ⇒) *ej* > *ý* in Gebauer 1963, 136 (cf. Marvan 1964) is well attested in Old Czech. The form *ty* is well-known also in South Polish dialects, cf. Klemensiewicz et al. 1964, 315 (the example *ty głupy babie* "to that dum hag"), and this is also the original, still-used form in Slovenian to the present day; the form *tej* is here an historical neologism (!), cf. Ramovš 1952, 88. It is not even possible to envisage the influence of the form *méj* < *méji* (< *mojeji*), for this is an equally secondary form following the primary form *mý,* cf. XII/4.5.

2.2   The form *dobřeji* could not contract, cf. XII/1.2.1, so that the new form *dobřéj, dobréj* — cf. Klemensiewicz et al. 1964, 333, Ramovš 1952, 104 — is not contracted, but secondarily modified. Its ending is as in the remaining forms reduced by one syllable and then lengthened. The problem of the longer forms of the type *dobřejeji* and their irrelevance was discussed in Chapter XII/4.3 and 4.7.

2.3   The forms *dobrý* — on the forms of modern Slovenian, cf. Ramovš 1952, 104 — and *tej/téj* must be taken as the consequence of integration in the whole central region of the expanded pair *tý/dobréj* — > *tý/téj/dobréj/dobrý.* In connection with this it is also possible to answer the question of the original quantity in the form *téj,* which is always problematical for Czech, cf. Vážný, 133. This ending shifted from the adjectival form *dobréj/dobréj* on the basis of such pairs as *dobré : té, dobrú : tú,* in which the endings fully agree; it is, therefore, evident that even in this position with an original contraction form there arose a pair with agreement of endings, i.e., *dobréj : téj,* so that the *téj* with length is primary.

2.4 Exactly like the form *tý* there developed also the form *mý* (< *méji* < *mojeji*), for whose second stage of contraction in M, cf. XII/4.5, there were no obstacles. In addition, compared to the form *tý,* it has the advantage that its paradigm ist still in much closer contact with the adjectival declension. However, on this see also 3.3!

3. SOME OLD CZECH DUAL FORMS OF THE PRONOUN *mojь (moji, moju/mú)*

3.0 Of the four forms of the dual Old Czech, Nom./Acc./ Voc. masc. *má* is contracted according to the ExD. *dobrá,* Dat./ Inst. *mýma* according to the ExD.*dobrýma;* No./Acc./Voc. fem./neut. *moji* is not contracted; there is vacillation in Gen./ Loc. *moju/mú.*

3.1 The form *moji* did not contract because it did not have an ExD; the corresponding form of the adjective, *dobřěji,* was itself incapable of contraction.

3.2 The doublet *moju/mú* we explain thus: the dual forms *tú, onú . . .* (< *toju, onoju . . .*), the only attested forms in Old Czech, cf. Vážný 1964, 133 ff., arose entirely regularly in M, for here D = 2. These forms serve in MM for contraction of the type *našeju > našú.* As was pointed out in Section 2, it is necessary in this possessive pronoun to conceive of two ExD. — adjectival and pronominal. The doublet *moju/mú* corresponds exactly to the following two interpretations:

1. *moju*   In. *mojь, moja, moji . . .*
      ExD. *tú, našú*
      ExG. *moja : ta, naša . . .*
2. *mú*   In. *má, mé, mégo . . .*
      ExD. *dobrú*
      ExG. *má : dobrá, mé : dobré . . .*

3.3 For the same reasons it would be possible to presume doublets of *mý : tý//méji : dobřěji.* Here, of course, it is the reverse situation: the expanded form is based on the adjective. This is, after all, delimiting even in the remaining forms that are much more frequent than the dual, like the Gen. sing, fem. *mé* and pl. forms of the type *mýchъ*, which are the only possible forms in Old Czech.

4. WEST SLAVIC *jí*, ACC. SING. MASC.

4.0 This form is attested for Czech, Vážný 1964, 119, Moravian Slovak, Stanislav 1958, 309, and Polish, Klemensiewicz at al 1964, 313. It is interpreted as *ji*, i.e., with short *i*. It is explained as a lengthening of *jь* to *ji* (cf. Old Church Slavic *i*, Nom. sing. masc. of the 3rd personal pronoun) or as a vocalization of (*jь* >)*i* with a secondary, morphological *j*- by analogy with the other forms, see Stanislav 1958, ibid., with bibliography. Vážný 1964, 123, also advocates the second position, whereas Klemensiewicz et al. 1964, ibid., merely state, *"ji"*, an archaic continuation of Proto-Slavic Acc. *jь*".

4.1 The change *jь* > *ji* is not possible even in this word-initial position, neither in Czech nor in other West Slavic languages. The change *jь* > *i* would be possible in Polish and Slovak (*j*- would here be a new morphological element), but in Czech, which has the most documents with the form *jí*, this change is precluded. Therefore, one speaks of vocalization, a change which, as in *toj* > *tej*, cannot be found outside of this case. It is obvious that these explanations were prompted by some perplexity over the interpretation of this form.

4.2.0 It appears that this perplexity is not necessary, if we here apply the explanation of contraction.

4.2.1 The form *jej* is the historically known, more modern doublet of this form. Vážný 1964, 124, together with Trávníček 1935, 362, derive this latter form from *ho* ~ (*jь* >) *j* : *je-ho* ⟹ *je-j*, i.e., the formation *je-* was extended into the Accusative.[1] The main objections to this hypothesis are chronological: the rise of the forms *ho, mu* is relatively recent, whereas **j* after the

---

[1] For another, quite remarkable explanation of the origin of this **je-** see Schmalstieg 1971, 133; his idea of the reduplicated paradigm of the pronoun **jь** fully supports our reconstruction in the following paragraphs.

fall of the jers (even in a form of the type *vɛ-t ъ-časъ > ve-t-čas)
is precluded, which the authors also assume.

4.2.2   It remains, therefore, to return to the premises which,
for example, Stanislav 1958, 309, advocates, that the form *jej*
reflects a reduplicated formation *jьjь*. The presupposition of the
existence of this formation means however, that it had to develop
as *jьjь* > *jí*, which is the explanation of the origin of this un-
explained form.

4.3   Objections to this interpretation can be reduced to
two major points:

1.   If the form did exist, it always had to contract before
the changes in the jers; that is to say, the system did not know
the combination *ьjь;* therefore, a form *jej* could not arise by
regular vocalization of the jers; where, then, is the proof that
jь jь existed at all?

2.   Word-initial *jь-* developed as *i-* in Polish and Slovak;
there arose a form *ijь*, which, when it survived, could not give *jej*.

4.3.1   A phonological model for *ьjь* actually did not exist,
but morphology can effect even those combinations that are alien
to phonology (cf. segments -é, -iu in Slovak, which are motivated
solely morphologically). Thus we have in Old Czech the form
otejdu, which, before the fall of the jers, still had the form
otъjьdǫ with the combination that the phonological system did
not know. It is, to be sure, possible and even probable that beside
this form there also existed a form *otýdǫ*, where *ý*, i.e., = ı, is
from *ъjь*. This form, though unattested (Old Polish *odydǫ*, cf.
Klemensiewicz et al. 1964, 114, is probably of different origin),
is, from data on the obligatoriness of P (cf. Chapter IV/3.2,
especially forms like *prídešь*, *výdešь*) quite certain; the existence
of the doublet *otejdǫ* : *otýdǫ* does not represent anything different
from the doublet *jej* : *jí*.

4.3.2   Word-initial *jь-* could be preserved for the same
morphological reasons; the form *jen* in Polish, after all, reflects
a form *jьnъ*, cf. Klemensiewicz et al. 1964, 114, similarly Stanislav 1958, 307. In sum, it can be said that phonetically regular
ijь would phonetically regularly coalesce into *i* (*j-* would here be
morphological); the morphologically motivated form *jьjь* would
be maintained uncoalesced for morphological reasons (or re-
duplication could be repeated, cf. Schmalstieg 1971) and would
develop into *jej* at the fall of the jers.

5. CONCLUSION

Analysis of contraction throws light also on certain unsolved concrete problems of declension. It was convenient to set forth earlier certain other questions of declension, forms like *dobrěji, moji, mojь* cf. XII/1.2, XI/2.4. The possibilities of analysis, of course, are not exhausted by this; for example, the conclusions of XV/1 can also be used in an investigation of the chronology of contraction, cf. XVII.

There are also cases to which it was here not possible to devote more attention and which deserve still further concrete investigation. Some concrete questions of other contraction languages — Slovenian and contiguous parts of Serbo-Croatian — seem to be particularly noteworthy in view of their proximity to West Slavic, cf. 1.1. Here belongs also the question of the inherited alternation motivated by contraction, *ej/ý* in Old Czech, cf. *tej/tý, otejdu/otýdu,* which could throw light on the problems of Old Czech diphthongization. The solutions of these interesting problems must await the investigations of others.

Even more can be gained from an investigation of conjugation than from an analysis of declension. We therefore devote the following chapter to this topic.

CHAPTER XVI

SPECIAL RECONSTRUCTION IN CONJUGATION

1. THE CHRONOLOGY OF THE RISE OF THE CONTRACTION CONJUGATION

1.0 The fact that contracted forms and uncontracted forms of the type *směješ se* : *smíš, děje se* : *dí, hraje* : *hrá*, etc. apparently are in free variation has led and continues to lead to skepticism regarding contraction as a single systemic process. Thus e.g., Mańczak 1966, 55 ff., attempts to explain exceptions in terms of lexical influences. If, in an alternation of this type, it is a matter of various word types or of word-type categories, i.e., of various morphological conditions, then an explanation, as a rule, is at hand, e.g, Komárek 1962, 46. Why, however, already asks Gebauer 1963, 555 ff.,[1] are there such differences as, e.g., *směš* "thou darest" : *směješ se* "thou laughest", etc. and he answers: "A different accent is the reason", *ibid.*, p. 557. However, as Komárek 1963, 730 in the same volume, warns, "Gebauer himself later (III/1, 579) limited the validity of his erroneous assumption that accent had an influence on coalescence". Gebauer's attempt at answering the question was abandoned without any other being made; Gebauer's question consequently remains unanswered.

1.1 It is indeed noteworthy how, e.g., Old Czech distinguishes doublets:

I.	II.
smě́š	*směješ sě*
tléš	*spěješ*
zráš	*hřěješ*
hráš, etc.	*baješ*, etc.

According to XIV/5, group I. represents the reflexes as they are in suffixed verbs, whereas group II. represents the reflexes of root verbs.

---

[1] This work was first puolished in 1894.

1.2 This means, therefore, that for group II, according to (14), in (TA)nI, n $>$ 1 applies, whereas for group I. n $=$ 1, is valid. Consequently the forms *smĕješь . . . *zraješь . . . could not exist, for they were not able to contract according to this principle. If contraction occurred here, then one more syllable had to be present in front of the contracting cluster.

1.3 If we examine this thesis against the etymology, we easily see that this is not in conflict with reality, for the forms of group I. did indeed have a jer in the first syllable, cf. sъmĕješь . . . zьraješь . . . , etc. so that the structure of these verbs corresponds to the structure of the suffixed verbs, whereas the forms of group II, like smĕješь sę, etc. (with no etymological jer) correspond to the structure of the root verbs.

1.4 By the fact that a necessary condition of contraction was the presence of a jer it is proven that the FALL OF THE JERS COULD HAVE OCCURRED ONLY AFTER CONTRACTION. This chronology will be the topic of the following chapter; in this chapter we shall focus on certain cases that apparently contradict these conclusions.

1.5 To such cases belongs the doublet dĕješ : dĕš, where the presence of a jer in the root is precluded, so that the previous explanation is not valid for it. This also applies to contracted forms with the Old Czech shape znáš, necháš, tráš, pláš, for which there is also doubt as to their being prefixed. We do not consider such pairs as hraješ : hráš, tleješ : tlíš, where Old Czech knows only the proper forms, and, further, cases of the type Polish znasz : poznajesz, umie : bieleje, etc., where it is clearly a question of territorial differences known from differences of the type umiesz : umiejesz, etc., cf. Klemensiewicz et al. 1964, 56, even though in these cases there is a need for further verification.

2. THE DOUBLETS dĕješ : dĕš

2.0 The present tense form dĕš . . . "thou sayest" is for the most part thought to be the outcome of the contraction of the forms dĕješ . . . , with parallel uncoalesced forms existing with the meaning "thou dost/makest", cf., e.g., Trávníček 1935, 398. Because, then, it is not a question of formal differences, i.e., phonological or morphological, for both forms have the same origin, the reason for this kind of divergent process is to be sought in that feature in which the two forms differ from each other, that is, in the region of semantics. Thus Trávníček 1935, *loc. cit.,* and already earlier Gebauer 1960, 222 ff., especially p. 228, where he retracts his explanation of the influence of a difference of stress on contraction in this verb. Most recently Mańczak 1966, who calls attention to the different frequency — the meaning "to speak" is much more frequent — attributes the differences to differences of the type Polish *dzie* "he says" : *dzieje (się)* "it happens", cf. p. 57, in addition to which, in connection with the question of frequency, he states beforehand on p. 55: "That is why verbs designating the action of speaking often undergo irregular phonetic abridgements, cf. Old Church Slavic *rьci,* Old Czech *dí < dějetь,* Russian *de,* Old Polish *pry < prawi, mówić < mołwić,,* Polish dial. *pada < powiada . . .*" But here it is necessary to proceed with caution: the case *rьci* belongs with cases of the type *pьci, žьdzi*; Russian *de* is not a verb form, but a particle, whose word-type function effected its weakening and irregular development; it is the same in this case also for Polish *pry* — which would be difficult without the connection with Czech *prý (< praví),* for Polish *pada,* cf. Czech dial. *poudá, povdá;* and finally, in Czech *čúš,* Polish *czusz (< čuješь) op. cit.* p. 57, there can also be no doubt about its adverbialization, i.e., its deparadigmatization. If Machek 1957, 302, is correct in stating that Polish *mówić, mowa* came from Ukrainian, then not even here would there be any question of claiming that *"l* fell out in rapid spech", *ibid.,* but on the loss of a geminated labial, which is foreign to the Ukrainian system, cf., e.g., Instr. *tińńu,* but *krowju,* in Borkovskij et al. 1963, 158. Cases of the type *déš* are in a completely different situation and must involve the development of the whole paradigm according to definite, strictly morphological rules which do not leave room for "irregularities" (why would the same semantic motivation not be valid for the 1st pers. sing. and the 3rd pers. pl.?). In connection with frequency, with which W. Mańczak has cited a number of interesting problems worthy of investigation, it is still necessary to call attention to the fact that high frequency weakens on the surface; however in the morphological plane, on the other hand, it conserves form, which is, for example, well known in the so-called "athematic" verbs, especially in the verb *byti, jesmь,* etc. Thus real weakening is usually connected with deparadigmatization or with change of function in general.

2.1 If the rule formulated in XVI/1 had to be valid even here, then in the form *déš* contraction would be excluded, and another explanation for this form would have to exist.

2.2 It is worthy of note that verbs contracted in the first historical phase of Old Czech still have relatively well attested 1st pers. sings. of the type *uměju, směju, dělaju, tbaju,* which gives evidence that the final stage of the integration of the contraction verbs with the athematic verbs, i.e., the penetration of the ending *-m* in the 1st pers. sing. into the contraction conjugation, is still in progress. Contrary to this, the form *dēju* in the meaning "I say" is not known at all, cf. Gebauer 1960, 228. Of course, certain other verbs, such as *jhráš, tléš,* do not have this expanded form attested either; but this is precisely in those cases in which the 1st pers. sing. is generally poorly attested, which does not come into consideration in the verb *dēti* "to say".

2.3 Even though this argument over the 1st pers. sing. in itself might lead to skepticism, it is nevertheless apparent that the form *dēm* must be treated more carefully. This means that one must consider other possibilities also, i.e., that we are dealing with an original form, one which the verb *dám, jēm* also originally had, consequently with a form ATHEMATIC by origin.

2.4 And now we shall combine these two considerations: according to 2.1; the former *déš* is not originally a *j*-stem verb (for then it would not have been able to contract); according to 2.3, there exists another explanation, i.e., athematicity; there is no other explanation, the form *dēm, déš* . . . must be athematic.

2.5 Objections can be only of a marginal nature, viz., the 3rd pers. pl. has the shape *dējú,* the imperative the shape *dēj* in contrast to *vēdē, vēz.* But already in the prehistoric period the whole athematic paradigm is under the powerful influence of the contraction paradigm, cf. the endings *-š* in the 2nd pers. sing., *-ø* in the 3rd pers. sing., the imperative *daj,* with which there is a similar situation also in the other languages, cf. Klemensiewicz et al. 1964, especially p. 362 ff., Belić 1962, v. 2, 56 ff., especially p. 67. In addition, this verb had at its disposal not merely a model, but the prepared form *dējú, dēj* in the formally close verb *d'áti* (< *dējati*).

2.6 Much more important than these marginal reservations is the fact that even earlier, apart from the problematics of contraction, there were reasons for assuming the athematicity of the conjugation of *děm, děš*. V. Machek reconstucts the Proto-Slavic doublet *dějǫ* : *děmь* "I put . . . I do : I say" on the formally and semantically perfect Hittite parallels *teḫi* : *temi* "I put : I say", cf. Machek 1957, 87, with further literature. This noteworthy hypothesis of a Hittito-Slavic isogloss has been almost universally passed over in silence by Slavists.[1] We find an uncertain allusion to the athematicity of *děm* in Belić 1962, v. 2, 56, where, in the section on athematic verbs under the paradigm of *jem, ješ*, we read the note: "The verb *děm* or *dim* is still of this type (i.e., like the verb *jem* — J.M.) in Čakavian speech". The necessary rehabilitation for this assumption is achieved by the investigation of contraction. The verb *děti* is the fifth — not counting *jьměti* — Slavic athematic verb.

3. THE RECONSTRUCTION OF THE VERB *znati*

3.0 Agreement with the Baltic forms, i.e., with Lithuanian *žinoti*, Latvian *zināt*, Old Prussian *-sinnat*, i.e., with Proto-Baltic *z'inā-*, in this verb was long ago rejected. Gebauer, on whose argument see 3.2, still adheres to this agreement. Like Old Church Slavic, Old Russian does not attest the corresponding form *zьnati*, but the form *znati*, which would correspond to an aorist stem, cf. Greek *égnōn*, cf. Machek 1957, 587.

3.1 The explanation for this Indo-European form is here somewhat weakened, for a velar would here already in Indo-European have occurred before a consonant and would consequently rather have had to develop as *g* in Slavic, not as *g' > z*, as Machek has several times pointed out: *op. cit.* in the entries *husa*, p. 151, *svekr*, p. 487, etc. Georgiev makes an appearance with a thought on this palatalization in 1932, cf. Georgiev 1958, where there is also a bibliography in which Machek is cited.

---

[1] Cf.., however Vjač, Vs. Ivanov: "Otraženije dvux serij indoevropejskix glagol'nyx form v praslavjanskom", **Slavjanskoje jazykoznanije**, V. V. Vinogradov et al., eds., Moscow 1968, p. 242f. with extensive literature, which indicates that the first to find this Czech-Hittite parallel was Bedřich Hrozný in 1917.

3.2.0   In Old Czech there are attested forms like *seznajúce,* *k rozeznáňú,* etc., cf. Gebauer 1963, 183-187, which lead him to the reconstruction of *seznati* (←*sъzьnati* and consequently *zьnati*). These arguments were seriously threatened by counter-arguments which the author adduces in the same passage: *ot znamení, v známost, sznamenal.* His arguments have thus sunk into oblivion.

3.2.1   However, it is worthy of note that this vocalization is not realized in nominal derivatives, especially those with the base *znamen-,* that for the most part it is not a question of prefixes, but prepositions, and that a case with an unvocalized prefix is not possible as a derivative of the verb *znati* (a form *sznati* is not attested) in the period of the vocalization of jers.

3.2.2   If Gebauer's explanation were shown to be correct, then it would be possible to explain the whole situation thus: the appropriate jer was preserved only in the most conservative conditions, both territorially — Czech and the surrounding area were non-innovative up to the period of contraction — and systemically — in the primary verb and verbs directly derived from it. Cases with prepositions could be more likely to undergo leveling. Cases with nominal stem could, in addition, undergo disetymologization and the fall of a jer could even depend on the division of the phrase. Doubts remain.

3.3   Let us now apply the results of XVI/1 to this form. Because, then, it is not a question of formal differences, i.e., concerned with suffixed verbs: consequently according to 1.2 and 1.3, the cluster *zn-* contained a jer. If we proceed from the facts of etymology, in the period of contraction, then this cluster had the form *zьn-* and the whole word the form *zьnati,* which corresponds fully to the Proto-Baltic form; therefore, we can designate it as Balto-Slavic.

3.4   Now let us consider once again the problem of Polish *poznajesz,* as was noted in 1.5. As Łoś 1927, 235, points out, this is a case of an originally perfective form; a doublet of the type *pozna : poznaje* cannot be interpreted as *da : daje* is interpreted; instead, it is a matter of the coexistence of two forms with the same function, i.e., a matter of fluctuation. Of course, this fluctuation does not concern only a single doublet, but the whole system, which depends upon dialectal differences, cf. Klemensiewicz et al. 1964, 56, Łoś 1927, 236, who characterizes

certain uncontracted forms as "an archaism or, rather, a pro-
vincialism". There is no doubt whatsoever that in the North
Polish dialects that lie in the periphery of the contraction territory suffixed verbs are not contracted. This property could assert
itself in the expressive type *bieleje;* in the type *poznaje* it was
adapted to the proportion *da : daje.* Serbo-Croatian *poznaješ,*
cf. Belić 1962, v. 2, 33, from which also in Serbo-Croatian
dialects forms like *skončaješ, puštaje,* etc. are known, cf. *ibid.*
p. 55, also respects this proportion, which is familiar in other
languages. On the periphery, which later phases of contraction
reached in a weakened form, the old conjugation system was able
to resist and to assert certain principles of its own.

4. THE WEST SLAVIC VERB *nechati*

4.0   In the verb *nechati* contraction takes place in the present
tense in West Slavic. This means that in that period this was a
suffixed verb, i.e., that the formation *ne-* is not morphologically
independent, but is a part of the root *nech-.*

4.1   This means that in this period there did not exist the
traditionally assumed simplex **chati,* as is inferred on the basis
of South Slavic *hajati,* cf., e.g., Stanislav 1956, 482, etc. Since
the contract is not shortened by prefixation, cf. Czech *neláti* in
contrast to *nebrati,* the form *nechati* cannot reflect **-chajati.*

4.2   Therefore it is necessary to assume that the South
Slavic forms without prefix are the result of secondary decomposi-
tion from *ne-chati,* to which the new simplex is adapted according
to the type *dajati, lajati, stajati . . . ,* in which in South Slavic
contraction does not occur.

4.3   Such systemic investigation can be used to confirm
the already existing hypothesis that the form *nechati* was primary
and that the South Slavic simplex is secondary. This notion is
cited, for example, by Machek 1957, 322, where there are some
attempts at a new etymology.

5. OLD CZECH *tráti,* SOUTH SLAVIC *trajati*

5.0   Contraction is assumed for this verb in Old Czech in
the present tense, cf., e.g., Trávníček 1935, 64 and 414. South
Slavic *trajati* leads to this interpretation.

5.1 However, Machek 1957, 538, who adduces the Old Czech doublets *trvati* : *tráti*, completely in agreement with our conclusions states: "The lack of 'uncoalesced' (*sic*) forms in Czech (*traje,* etc.) shows that there was no old *tra-ja-ti*", so that "there is no doubt that *trvati* is the more nearly original form, whereas *tráti*, etc. developed from it by abbreviation in the course of the rapid tempo of speech (after all, *r* was non-syllabic in Czech) . . . "

5.2 In reference to this it would be possible to make the following observations: the form *trvati* is inarguably primary, as shown by the etymology, but not in the New Czech form, i.e., not with $r̥$, but with $r̥$, and that is in agreement with the fact that here the reflex of the form *trъvati* is under consideration; the forms *trvati* : *tráti* arose from this form by parallel development.

5.3 The rise of these parallel forms bears upon a process of dephonologization of the opposition, syllabicity of sonorant : non-syllabicity of sonorant. This process, slipping into Czech in the 14th century, was realized so that it interfered with the possibility of the occurrence of non-syllabic sonorants in positions where a syllabic sonorant was also possible, i.e., in an inter-consonantal position. Hence, for the form *tr̥vati* (cf. New Polish *tr̥wać*) there were two ways to realize this dephonologization: either by the syllabicization of the sonorant, i.e., $TR̥T > TR̥T$, or by the elimination of the interconsonantal position, i.e. $TR̥T > TR$. From the first process there arose *trvati*, from the second, *tráti*. This dephonologization motivated a similar split in a number of other cases, e.g., *zrzavý* : *rzavý, jablko* : *jabko,* etc.

5.4 Because even on South Slavic territory $r̥/r̥$ were dephonologized in a similar way (the case *gr̥oce, umr̥o* in Serbo-Croatian are only secondary), they can be accounted for by an analogical process. The form *trajati* arises analogically like *hajati*, cf. 4.2, or in the words of Machek 1957, *ibid.,* "in Bulgarian and Serbo-Croatian, then, *tra-* tended toward the type *la-ja-ti.*"

5.5 The form *tráš*, consequently, did not rise by contraction from **traješ*, but its rise had the following stages: *trъvaješъ > trъváš̌ъ > tr̥váš > tráš*, thus: 1) contraction, necessary in a suffixed verb, 2) loss of jers, dephonologization of the opposition $r̥ : r̥$. Without the assumption that contraction preceded the fall of the jers, the development in this verb is not even conceivable.

136

6. THE PRESENT TENSE OF OLD CZECH *pláti*

6.0   Even the forms *pláš, plá* . . . in Old Czech are not contracted forms; rather, they are secondary.

6.1   The original pair *polti* : *pol'ǫ,* by methathesis split into *plati* : *pol'ǫ,* which is the opposition preserved in Slovene *plati* : *poljo* and Old Czech *kláti* : *kol'u.* The original present tense form of the verb *pláti* was not preserved in Old Czech.

6.2   It is obvious that the new present tense form arose on the basis of the infinitive in accordance with the pairs *znáti* : *znáš, jhráti* : *jhráš,* etc. In addition, investigation of contraction establishes the chronology of this inception: contact between *pláti* and the type *znáti* could have occurred only after the fall of the jers, when it had ceased to hold good that one syllable had to precede the contract in the present tense. Consequently, the structure of *pláti* could be interpreted in the same way as the infinitives of verbs of the type *znáti,* which thus could provide a convenient model for the formation of the new present tense *pláš.*

PART FOUR

THE ROLE OF CONTRACTION
IN FURTHER DEVELOPMENT

CHAPTER XVII
CONTRACTION AND THE FALL OF THE JERS
(JER SHIFT):
THE CHRONOLOGY AND ITS SIGNIFICANCE

1. OBSERVATIONS ON CHRONOLOGY
THE PROBLEM OF CENTRAL SLOVAK.

1.0   Gebauer in his time attempted to establish the chronology of contraction, although he was content to use the Old Czech
přehláska (umlaut) of *'a* > *ě* as a *terminus ante quem* as proof of
age. He writes of contraction: ". . . it is of very ancient origin.
For example, *státi* was contracted from *stojati* before the *přehláska* of *a* to *ě,* i.e., before the 12th century . . ." (cf. Gebauer
1963, 563).

1.1   "This analysis" of Gebauer's "can be accepted even
today; however probably *(sic)* it is necessary to shift contraction
back to before the changes in the jers", says Komárek 1962, 46,
of our contraction. Whereas Gebauer's chronology is certain, thís
new hypothesis is subsequently formulated as merely "probable".

1.2   Trubetzkoy 1929 appears as the first with an idea on
the chronology of 1) contraction, 2) the fall of the jers. His
authority here, however, met with objections. The argument adduced by him — *prišьstvьje* > Old Czech *příště,* where vocalization
of the even-numbered jer did not occur because contraction had
been realized in front of it — is refuted by the fact that the
final jer stood in tense position (before *j*) and was not, consequently, able to fulfil the function of an odd-numbered jer:
"It may be assumed that already, before the fall and vocalization
of the jers, *ьj, jь* had changed to *ii* . . ." (cf. Pauliny 1963, 97).
It was demonstrated in J — cf. XI/1 — that the difference
between *ьj* and *ij* is not irrelevant and that in the cluster *ьj* the
jer behaves like every odd- numbered jer, i.e., it vanishes, in
a different way, of course, so that the hypothesis the author
cited of a merger of *ь* and *i* in tense position is not applicable.
This, however, does not entirely exclude the possibility that the

tense position might make it impossible for the jer to perform its function, i.e., to vocalize a preceding jer. For this reason, a similar unvocalized case, *ogъbъje* > Old Czech *ohbě* also meets with the same objection in Komárek 1962, cf. also Bernštejn 1968, 29.

1.3 Trubetzkoy's hypothesis receives much more support from the development of the pair *stryjьcь/ujьcь* > *strýc/ujec*, cited in Komárek 1962, 47. Where contraction occurred in the first word, in the second word vocalization of the jers was realized, which excludes the conception of the development *jь* > *i* cited in Pauliny 1963 and excludes it for all contraction languages. We know, however, that the change in the first case is spontaneous, being realized without hindrances of any kind, that it is a primary process, that it is some kind of forerunner of the whole process; by this means, therefore, the conception in Trávníček 1935 that contraction and the fall of the jers are "virtually simultaneous phenomena" cannot be refuted, cf. *ibid.* p. 68.

1.4 Not even analysis of the development of forms of the type *ovьčьjь* can solve the problem. It would be expected that the first *ь* would have to be vocalized in the major number of the forms, i.e., *oveč(ь)ja, oveč(ь)je*, etc. However, this is true only in East Slavic, cf. Russian *ovečij*. Not only in West Slavic, but also in the South Slavic territory, the vocalization is unknown, not only, e.g., in Štokavian, where it is *ovči*, but also in Bulgarian, where it is the same unvocalized form, *ovči*. Here, of course, there can be no question of contraction; the lack of vocalization is consequently motivated by the special position of the following jer.

1.5 Despite these difficulties and special — as it appears, not entirely cogent — reservations, Pauliny 1963 leans toward Trubetzkoy's conception for the whole of West Slavic except Central Slovak, where, on the contrary, he assumes that the fall of the jers occurred before contraction. His hypothesis of aberrations in the development of Central Slovak he bases on the following arguments, cf. *ibid.*, p. 97 ff. and Bernštejn's (1968, 27) support:

1. Changes of the forms *ženojǫ, tojǫ*, etc.: a diphthong could arise in a contraction only after denasalization and consequently only after the fall of the jers, which preceded denasalization.

2. Central Slovak, in contrast to the other West Slavic languages, did not use variants of the *é* that arose on contraction as alternatives to jers.

3. Central Slovak produced the rhythmic law, thanks precisely to this peculiar chronology; after the fall of the jers, differences of intonation were revalued into differences of quantity, so that after a long syllable there always followed a short one. This model was then obligatory even for the later contraction, so that a long syllable after a long syllable was shortened.

1.6 However, on all these points of the argument different possibilities can be adduced:

1.a. denasalization may have occurred before the fall of the jers, which even Pauliny 1963, 100, concedes;

b. the contraction *ojǫ* > *ǫ́* is not a phonetic change; it can be realized only with the participation of morphological factors, cf. IX/1.4, 7, especially, however, XV/1. The lack of morphological factors can tell us nothing about the chronology of contraction;

c. all of Slovenian and part of Serbo-Croatian know contraction, cf. Ramovš 1952, 58 ff.; this would mean, therefore, that these dialects have the same chronology as West Slavic; Central Slovak, then, with the rest of the Serbo-Croatian dialects, has the opposite;

d. the change of *oju* > *ou* is not a contraction but rather a later development, where intervocalic *j* has obviously disappeared.

2.a. It is true that those contraction dialects that know *é* reflect *ъ* as *e*, i.e., *ъ/ь* as +*é*; this concerns also Slovenian and Serbo-Croatian dialects; but this does not argue against anything, for in Central Slovak and Štokavian *ó* arose in these positions, IX/1.4, 6'; this, doubtless, relegates Central Slovak to the South Slavic periphery, but it does not preclude a common chronology;

b. in the dialects of Styrian Slovene south of the Mura River, there are the forms *dobroga, dobromu*, but there is development of both jers into +*e* even here, cf. Ramovš 1935, 183, 191; the reason for this development must lie, therefore, in the dephonologization of the opposition *ъ/ь*;

c. the fact that Central Slovak, in contrast to all other contraction languages and in conformity with the non-contraction languages, reflects ъ > *o* may, therefore, be due to the fact that this phonological opposition survives here.

3.a.   Chronology cannot be deduced from the rhythmic law itself; it may also be a part of entirely different factors, cf. here, e.g., XVIII/4;

b.   the rise of the new category of quantity on West Slavic territory and the subordination of the old prosodic relationships also concern Central Slovak; it would be more than surprising that this dialect should here follow different routes to the same goals.

1.7   The traditional hypothesis on the very specific development of the Central Slovak contraction is rather superannuated and is still repeated, cf. Pauliny 1963, 98 ff. Pauliny latched on to this tradition and explained further facts from its point of view. He did so perfectly legitimately, for he was aware of the liability of a hypothesis based originally on the different nature of the single contraction cluster *oją*. Theoretically there are, according to table 9, $8^2 = 64$ possible contraction clusters; usually, only 15 to 20 examples are adduced, only those, of course, that have contracted; there are, however, more than 30 clusters that actually existed prior to contraction, without regard to their reflexes. This overwhelming preponderance of consistencies against a single incosistency itself urges caution upon the investigator. The possibility of a different explanation was shown and proved in XV/1.

2.   THE PRIORITY OF CONTRACTION

2.0   In spite of the difficulties, adduced, it was necessary to work with the hypothesis that contraction occurred before the fall of the jers. If it were a matter of concern to us that contraction be explained as a relatively compact process on the whole of contraction territory, it would be necessary to exclude a hypothesis on specific features in the chronology of Central Slovak. Taken to its logical conclusion, even on South Slavic territory we would find ourselves faced with the same paradox, cf. 1.5.1.

2.1   This chronology was especially important for the establishment of the chronological and typological character of

J as the last stage and for the explanation of the non-realization of contraction in cases where $A^2 = \text{ь}$, cf. XI/2.3.-5.

2.2 Not even continuity and chronological and typological harmony, of course, yield a completely certain hypothesis; every acceptable hypothesis — if it is not a matter of out-and-out provisional arrangement — must, to a certain exent, have harmony. It was a question of whether Trubetzkoy's chronology could be proved by other means that would exclude the objections of XVII/2.

2.3 Already in XII/3, in the reconstruction of the opposition $T^-é$: $T'ě$, which arose in contraction (in cases like, e.g., *dobré* : *pěšě*), it was found that the variant *é* is tied to T^+. The fact that *é* outside of this position arose only by compensatory lengthening, i.e., by processes chronologically subsequent to the fall of the jers indicates that the phenomena of contraction appeared in the system earlier than this fall of the jers occurred.

2.4 The task of the preceding chapter was to give completely evident proof for this chronological line of argument. In XVI/1, especially 1.2, 1.3, it was shown that a necessary condition for contraction was, in certain verbal forms, the presence of a vowel, even of the kind of vowel that it is necessary to reconstruct as a jer. After the fall of the jers, at least, in those verbal cases, contraction could not have occurred. Because in this direction contract languages develop compactly, we must state that the whole of contraction territory developed in a continuous manner, therefore, in essence, before the fall of the jers. Thus, our conclusions from XVII/1 are also demonstrated.

2.5 Because the conditions for contraction in the presence of jers concern MF and M, while J, under the same conditions, had to have begun earlier than the end of MM, cf. XI/2.3, we have at our disposal a relatively exact chronology for the beginning of the fall of the jers. At the moment of the completion of M, this process (J) had not been carried through as a whole, while in the period of MM it was already operating.

2.6 By these findings we attain as well an absolute chronology of contraction. The fall of the jers began in Slovenian and Polish in the 10th century (cf. Shevelov 1964, 458 f.). The process of contraction could have begun to be realized only in the second half of the 9th century, so that it was realized in the course of a single century, cf. XIX, table 13.

2.7   Firm establishment of the chronological relationship between contraction and the fall of the jers also makes it possible to explain certain further problems, particularly the significance of contraction for the further development of the system. This will be the subject of these concluding chapters.

3.   THE INFLUENCE OF CONTRACTION ON THE FALL OF THE JERS. TWO TERRITORIAL SOURCES OF THEIR FALL.

3.0   If we proceed from the chronology in 2.5, then it is necessary to assume that in Bulgarian and Macedonian the fall was realized at the same time as in contraction territory, or, perhaps, even somewhat earlier.

3.1.0   Generally, it is recognized that the fall of the jers is the consequence of their reduction. However, Bulgarian is characterized by the fact that this surface motivation can be retarded, modified, and paralyzed by the constraints of the system. i.e., that the jers cannot disappear regardless of circumstances, cf. Mirčev 1963, 110 ff., further Shevelov 1964, 448 ff.

3.1.1   One of the constraints is the systemic rule of open syllables. In an inscription from Preslav from the 10th century, ь is always written for both jers at the end of a word, cf. Mirčev 1963, 110. The author regards this as proof that here it is only a matter of a traditional grapheme without phonetic value, that consequently in this position in that period the jers had already fallen. However, there is also a different possibility: the jers were neutralized here as a result of their reduction; however, they retained their vocalic value, so that the original structure of the syllable was preserved.

3.1.2   The validity of this assumption of neutralization is confirmed also by other cases of the preservation of weak jers, those in inlaut, cf. *dъska* > *dăska, tъko* > *tăka//tьma* > *tăma, žьnǫ* > *žana*. In these cases, where both jers likewise develop in the same way, it was a matter of the original structure of the syllable accepting only specific consonantal combinations. The system resisted new combinations by preserving a jer vowel; but since the jer was weak, the system further weakened it to a minimum and neutralized the opposition ъ : ь.

3.1.3   The morphological system also resisted the fall of the jers. If certain forms of a paradigm contained a strong jer, e.g., *sъnъ*, then the jer was also retained in other forms, e.g., *sъna*. The morphological system here strove for the retention of the isomorphic form. Only certain cases from the preceding paragraph could be included here; in them we must consider the neutralization of jers. Resistance in the face of homonymity, as in *săvĕt : svĕt*, also is included in the morphological constraints; in some cases it is, of course, a matter of secondary restoration.

3.2 We state, therefore, that the reduction of jers, leading to their loss, met with sharp resistance from the system and that it overcame this resistance only gradually and inconsistently. This phenomenon concerns the whole of South Slavic and perhaps partially East Slavic besides, cf. on this also Bernštejn 1961, 249, and Isačenko 1970.

3. In contrast to this, West Slavic — outside of the Polabian region, which we have not taken into our consideration — is characterized by absolute consistency in the changes in the jers. Is it possible to find its relationship to contraction?

3.4 In XIII there were stated certain results of contraction, of which the following will interest us:

1. The destruction of the integrity of the old syllable: the vowel develops independently of the preceding consonants or cluster of consonants.

2. Thus there arises the new category of the softness correlation of consonants, cf. XIII/4.

3. On this new category also depends the existence of the variant *é* over the greater part of contraction territory XIII/3.

4. As a result of the presence of ι in the system, the opposition *ь/ъ : i/y* cannot be treated as a quantitative opposition and the jers lose their fundamental systemic relationship, see XIII/2.

3.5 The most important consequences of the fall of the jers for the phonological system were the loss of the old syllable structure and the development of the softness correlation. But, according to 3.4, 1-3, neither of these features is a consequence of the fall of the jers; this process only completed them, extending their validity even beyond the contraction syllable. That is, closed syllables and the correlation extends even to new positions, especially to the absolute end of a word.

3.6 This means that the reduction fo jers in West Slavic was not the cause of their loss, but only a prerequisite of this process. The loss was here realized consistently, thanks to the fact it did not have any systemic constraints as there were, e.g., in Bulgarian; also, in the case of the jers, it was not only a question of phonetic reduction, but also of systemic weakening in the aftermath of the rise of modern quantity, cf. 3.4.4.

3.7 All contraction languages that evolved the variant $^-é$ used it for the reflex of strong ъ. Here, of course, we have to bear in mind the dephonologization of the opposition ъ/ь into one phoneme which can be designated by $^+ə$, which made possible the development $^+ə > ^+e$ over the whole of the territory with the variant é.

3.8 We therefore explain the fall of the jers as a parallel process with two sources. The first source was the South-East Slavic region, where only the extrasystemic conditions leading to reduction of the jers were the impetus for change and where the system resisted this more or less successfully. The other source of this development in the jers was the focus of contraction, where systemic underlying factors resulting from contraction also fell in with the surface impulses, cf. 3.4. These factors caused the spread of a much more energetic and consistent process, which knew no exceptions.

3.9 On South Slavic territory these processes conflicted, with almost all contraction languages realizing both jers as one phoneme — something entirely foreign to non-contraction languages. On South Slavic contraction territory, however, there was carried out such an important feature of South-East Slavic origin, the vocalization of jers in initial syllables. The data of contraction show that these streams from two sources conflicted in the region between Čakavian and Štokavian. J probably penetrated into Štokavian, cf. Shevelov 1964, 528. Slovenian does not provide a clear picture; "uncontracted" forms like (*korvьjь, gostьje, smerčьje* >) *kravji, gostje, smrečje,* etc. are current, but here further dialectological investigation is necessary. The vocalization of the jers cited nevertheless covered the whole of South Slavic territory, cf. *op. cit.* p. 449 ff., especially the table on p. 451.

3.10 The concept of two sources for the fall of the jers is not unconnected with social conditions. Both sources lie on the territory of old political and cultural centers of the Slavs, with good possibilities of contacts with Slavic neighbors.

3.11 The dynamic isogloss of loss of jers penetrates into East Slavic much later. With regards to the fact that there it is connected with the softness correlation of consonants, as was the case in West Slavic, it is possible to assume that it penetrated from the West. But is Church Slavic the only South Slavic component of this development? East Slavic deserves still further attention in regard to this question.

3.12 Contraction, this embryonic disjunctive change, not only preceded the fall of the jers, but also energetically carried through this last Common-Slavic change.

CHAPTER XVIII

LOCAL VARIANTS IN THE DEVELOPMENT

1. DIFFERENCE IN WEST SLAVIC AND SOUTH SLAVIC DUE TO CONTRACTION

1.0 From the beginning of our investigation of contraction there have been many opportunities of differentiating the contraction territory according to intensity of development. These differences concern chiefly the phonological system. In this, it was not only a question of differences among the focus, the central region, and the periphery: Štokavian, e.g., developed on the periphery, where it was not even possible to place a definite boundary between contraction territory and non-contraction territory, cf. III/4.3.

1.1 Certain features distinguish this dialect from those of the remaining South Slavic contraction territory. These are chronologically older features. Chronologically younger features unite the whole of South Slavic contraction territory and distinguish it from West Slavic territory. Central Slovak behaves similarly compared to West Slavic; on specific relationships to the South Slavic region, see XVIII/2.

1.2 The role of contraction in the rise of the West Slavic softness correlation is obvious. On South Slavic territory the rise of this category is noticeably weakened; in MF *sějati > s'áti* does not contract here (of this negative process on Slovak territory there is not even a trace! Cf. Stanislav 1958, 503), which is an important step for the rise of the softness correlation. Here morphological factors also collaborated, viz., the absence of contraction in the infinitive of the type *lajati*. A large part of South Slavic territory, however, carried out the rise of the variant *é;* but a real breakthrough into the system and the establishment of the softness correlation could only be expected from J in this situation. It is possible that not only Čakavian, but also the whole of Slovenian realized this stage, but without the consequences that contraction had on West Slavic territory. Of course, the consequence are typically South Slavic — the new phonological features had to adapt to the old system.

1.3   The principal difference between South Slavic and West Slavic contraction territory is, therefore, that on West Slavic territory contraction brought fundamental systemic changes to the phonology, whereas on South Slavic territory the results of contraction had to adapt to the old phonological system.

1.4   At the same time, the differences concern not only the softness correlation, but also the direct results of contraction — the contract and its quantity. This new quantity became the basic prosodic principle of West Slavic, influencing the stabilization of the stress, cf. XVIII/2i, on South Slavic territory, it adapted itself according to the old prosodic relationships.

1.5   Did there exist here, then, the phonological opposition $y : i$ or were these variants of one phoneme, as was the case in the West Slavic languages? The common results of vocalization point to the second possibility. However, because for the most part, $T^- : T'$ was not valid — cf. 1.2 — then, after the loss of the phonological distinction they also had to lose the phonetic distinction, after the loss of systemic differences they also had to lose surface differences, both vowels also merged into one phonetically. The common reflex of the two jers would indicate that this process was realized even before the fall of the jers.

1.6   We can, therefore specify the thesis that the two influences of the fall of the jers overlapped on South Slavic territory. The South Slavic territory with the variant $é$ partially — together with West Slavic — used it as the reflex of both jers, whereas Štokavian used a. Central Slovak here, therefore, developed beyond the region of South Slavic; ъ/ь had to be at least variants.

2.   OUTLINE OF THE RISE OF THE NEW PROSODIC FEATURES OF WEST SLAVIC

2.0   The rise of West Slavic quantity cannot be separated from the rise of the phonological category of contract. No one rejects this relationship, but neither is anyone investigating it more closely. The consequences of contraction are, of course, the most important common isoglosses of the West Slavic languages, much more important both as to phenomena and as to system than is the development of the clusters *dj, tj,* or *bj, pj* . . . , cf. I/3, the preservation of the clusters *dl, tl,* cf. I/4, especially 4.7, 4., etc.

2.1   Only the contraction languages retained phonological quantity. In the sense of 1.3 and 1.4, South Slavic develops toward the preservation of the old relationships, West Slavic toward their suppression and the installation of the new prosodic relationships motivated by contraction. The question is, what course did this installation take? We shall attempt to outline this process very briefly in the following paragraphs.

2.2   It is assumed that the revaluation of the old prosodic relationships was realized after the fall of the jers, cf. Pauliny 1963, 142, Horálek 1962, 139, etc. This assumption, from the point of view of contraction, can be formulated thus: the building up of the softness correlation is directly conected with the rise of contraction, cf. 1.2, so that the softness correlation had validity primarily only in the position before $\bar{A}$, therefore, in a contraction syllable. Thus, the contraction syllable represented within the system an autonomous unit in which, and only in which, there were realized obligatorily and inseparably two new phonological features — the softness correlation and modern quantity. The opposition

$$T'\bar{A} : T^-\bar{A} \tag{18}$$

is valid for all T and all $\bar{A}$; it has, therefore, general validity. This does not mean that outside of opposition (18) any kind of softness opposition was excluded. There had already existed for a long time pairs of the type *ĺa : la* . . . , *ŕa : ra* . . . , *ńa : na* . . . , but these did not themselves suffice for the carrying out of the softness correlation of consonants as a pan-systemic principle. Under the influence of the opposition $T'i : T^-\acute{y}$, in which, according to (18), $i/\acute{y}$ are only variants, the opposition $T'i : T^-y$, and further $T'ь : T^-ь$ point to the same result. This is the first step, when the new principle also actively asserts itself beyond the boundaries of the contraction syllable. It is the first step because (18) is always generally valid only for contraction syllables, whereas it is only partially valid otherwise. With the loss of the jers this extraterritoriality of the contraction syllable within the old system was lost; the old and the new systems, whose coexistence had up till then had an autonomous character, came into contact and therefore also into conflict.

2.3 The modern opposition Ā : A achieved unlimited scope. Both correlates had homogenous properties: in the word they were independent of position and in principle also of stress, cf. on this also 2.6. The old opposition *acute : circumflex,* which we write as Aa : Ac, had different homogenous properties: dependence upon position in the word — the vowel had to be long, which was excluded in certain positions — and upon stress.

The opposition Ā : A, therefore, was realized in the following cases (where +, — means possibility/impossibility of realization respectively):

	Long	Short
Stressed	+	+
Unstressed	+	+

TABLE 12

whereas the opposition Aa : Ac was realized in the following cases:

	Long	Short
Stressed	+	—
Unstressed	—	—

TABLE 12'

The fact that the opposition Aa : Ac was limited only to a relatively narrow range of possibilities, whereas the opposition Ā : A was realized practically without limit, decided the conflict between the old and the new systems; the opposition with general validity prevailed.

2.4 This general West Slavic scheme obviously had various local modifications, as the individual West Slavic languages and dialects indicate; however, the core of the process was realized in this direction.

2.5   The connection of the rise of the new quantity with the fixing of stress is as obvious as it is unclear in concrete features. We propose the following hypothesis without binding ourselves to it in any manner: jers could not be the bearers of stress because of their unique position in the system, that of reduced vowels; the stress in such cases was shifted forward one syllable. The new phonological category of contract likewise occupied a unique position in the system: the contraction syllable forms within the word an extraterritorial unit; it would not be the bearer of old prosodic relationships like the intonation of long stressed syllables. Therefore this syllable also shifted the stress one syllable forward, insofar as this was possible; however, the stress could not be shifted in cases of the type *zъlý, ně, láti,* so that this assumption does not contradict the conception in 2.3. This shift, which chiefly concerns final syllables — practically the whole *morphological* category of contract — affects the whole phonological and morphological system. The tendency to relieve from stress all endings (cf. the analogous process in Štokavian, though not in Čakavian), i.e., the bearer of stress had to be the stem of the word, could have played a deciding role. And that was the first step toward the stabilization of the stress.

3.   THE PLACE OF CENTRAL SLOVAK FROM THE POINT OF VIEW OF CONTRACTION

3.0   It is not possible to deny certain South Slavic features of Central Slovak. The question is what light the results of the investigation of contraction can cast on them.

3.1.0   Bernštejn 1961, 79-80 *passim,* attempts a concrete formulation of the South Slavisms in this West Slavic dialect by means of a theory of a Slovenian-Slovak isogloss region that was characterized by the activity of the South Slavic partner. From this activity the West Slavic partner acquires the following features:

1.   the South Slavic development of the circumflexed word-initial clusters *ort-, olt-*
2.   the second palatalization of $x > s$
3.   the development of *r'*
4.   the ending *-ou* in the Instrumental sing (chiefly in fem.) of the type *rukou*

5. the absence of palatalization in the Dat./Loc. sing. fem. of the type *ruke*

6. the loss of the Vocative

7. the Dat./Loc. of personal pronouns of the type *tebě, sebě* in contrast to the West Slavic type *tobě, sobě*

8. the ending *-mo* in the 1st pers. pl. Pres.

3.1.1 Features 1-3, 7, 8, however connect Central Slovak with the whole South Slavic territory (and with at least one non-South Slavic language), so that features 4-6 have to attest to specific Slovenian-Slovak relationships. The ending *-ou* from *-ojǫ,* however, did not arise in Slovenian; the Styrian forms *-om, ou,* etc. are only secondary, cf. Ramovš 1952, 58 ff; the latter is, on the other hand, typical for Štokavian. The absence of palatalization of the type *roke* is not generally Slovenian; it is the the northern Carinthian dialects which have palatalization here, cf., *op. cit.,* the examples on p. 57; nor does palatalization always occur in Serbo-Croatian; features 2 and 5 are mutually contradictory by the fact that there exist in Central Slovak forms of the type *muse;* these forms exclude point 5 from consideration: a number of so-called South Slavisms are in fact the result of a much later development where South Slavic is excluded, cf. on this in general outline Pauliny 1963, 36 f., 44 f., and Horálek 1962, 398: "secondary parallels". The situation is similar also in the Vocative, cf., e.g., Ramovš 1952, 40.

3.1.2 The development of *g* to a voiced velar spirant is pointed to as an indication of Central Slovak influence on Slovenian and the development *tl > tl/l* is pointed to as an indication of their reciprocal influence. But the first case can also be a matter of a Czech-Slovenian isogloss — after all, it is precisely these contacts that can be demonstrated for the period of contraction, cf., e.g., III/7, diagram 1 — and even in the second, chronologically totally different case, the same interpretation is at least equally germane; it is fundamental here that Slovak has no forms with *kl/gl* (secondary Slovak forms of the type *glhý,* in which changes occur before *l,* are foreign to South Slavic and are obviously later, cf. Pauliny 1963, 169) and that the vacillation between *tl/dl* and *l,* as it is known from Slovenian, cannot be demonstrated. Slovenian here exhibits a transistory character; in Central Slovak it is a matter of a South Slavism without closer specification.

154

3.1.3 The effort to specify the thesis of Central Slovak South Slavisms is a service that, in Bernštejn 1961, can only be welcomed. However, it is not possible to realize it by the application of Slovenian data.

3.2.0 The ending -*ou* is on South Slavic territory typical not of Slovenian, but on the contrary, of certain Serbo-Croatian dialects, especially extreme peripheral štokavian. Of course, the rise of this ending did not have phonetic reasons, but morphological ones, cf. XV/1, where the territorial extent of this change is also discussed.

3.2.1 There is one more outstanding feature of Central Slovak that confirms the possibility of its contact with štokavian. This is the absence of the variant ⁻*é*, which so conspicuously distinguishes both these dialects from the whole of the remainder of contraction territory as is especially apparent in its morphological consequences, cf. the type *dobró, dobrógo* . . . and the absence of contraction in the type *moje, mojego.*

3.2.2 Both dialects are likewise distinguished from the remainder of contraction territory by the specific development of the jers.

3.3 These isoglosses, applied to the question of the position of Central Slovak, refer this dialect not only to the periphery, but specifically to the South Slavic periphery. Because Kajkavian belongs at this stage to Slovenian and Čakavian also adjoins it, Central Slovak must lie to the east of Čakavian in this period, i.e. in the period of contraction. On the assumption that the Slovenian dialect then constituted a continuum, the southern section of the contraction territory can, on the basis of III/7, diagram 1, be specified thus:

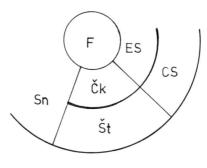

DIAGRAM 2

F = Focus, i.e., Czech with West Slovak
Sn = Slovenian, including Kajkavian
Čk, Št = Čakavian, Štokavian
ES, CS = East Slovak, Central Slovak

Beyond the outer limit lies the South Slavic transperiphery.

3.4   The assumption of an original contact of Central Slovak with the eastern portion of South Slavic territory would be confirmed by the form *oni sa,* which is also known from Macedoian. The jers are also vocalized in the same manner, i.e. *ь* > *e, ъ* > *o,* e.g. *dьnь* > Slovak *deň,* Mac. *den, prědъkъ* > Slovak, Mac. *predok* (cf. Shevelov 1964, 453). The third isogloss shared by Slovak with the Macedonian(-Bulgarian) area is the development of the negative form *nejesmь* > *něsmь* > Slovak *nie som* which can be only slightly older than the contraction in other cases (cf. the regular development in Czech *neje* > *ně* in this form only).

Summing up all these data the conclusions are the following:

a.   the bearers of the Central Slovak dialect were leaving their original South Slavic sites (cf. diagram 2) at the time when the jers began to fall, cf. the Slovak-Macedonian isoglosses;

b.   they reached their (North) Pannonian sites in about 100 years and established intensive contacts with the West Slavic (primarily future West and East Slovak) dialects, cf. the West Slavic distribution of the jer vocalization (weak jers are regularly dropped; for *teraz* see cb.);

c.   between these two extreme chronological points two geographically obvious intermediate stages must be constructed:

ca.   the contact with the Štokavian area, which is proved by two chronologically, territorially and formally dependable isoglosses, i.e. *ojǫ* > *ou* (see 3.2.0) and *dobroje, dobrajego* > *dobró, dobrógo;* this explains also the third isogloss, i.e. numerous cases in which (as in Štokavian both jers are vocalized into *a,* e.g. *mъchъ* > *mach* (Štok. *mah*), *chrьbъtъ* > *chrbát* (Štok. *hrbat*) etc.

cb.   the contact with the North Slovenian dialect, cf. the rhythmic law (see XIII/4) and exceptional cases in which a weak jer in the first syllable is vocalized: *tъraz* > *teraz* (*ъ* > *e* excludes Štokavian or Macedonian contacts.

Thus the development from the end of the 9th century to the end of the 10th century can be constructed as follows:

1. the contact with the Macedonian(-Bulgarian) area (*oni sa,* ъ > *o, nie som*)

2. the contact with the Štokavian area (*ou, oje* > *ó, ъ/ь* > *a*)

3. the contact with North Slovenian dialects (rhythmic law, *teraz,* etc., see below)

4. the contact with West Slavic, West and East Slovak dialects (West Slavic development of the contraction and the jers).

The sequence of these four stages, although each of them quite well represents one generation, should not be interpreted discretely but rather as a continuous development. There was probably no clear cut division between them, and the relations should be understood as bilateral contacts (e.g. Mac — Slovak — Štok, Štok — Slovak — Slovenian) with a gradual weakening of the southern contacts and strengthening of the northern ones.

4. Remarks on the rhythmic law

4.0 The important attempt at an historical interpretation of the Central Slovak rhythmic law in Pauliny 1963, 141 ff., which is based on the thesis of a specific chronological contraction in this dialect, is not, according to XVII, applicable.

4.1 It is not, of course, certain when this law arose; if there is no chronology, we cannot investigate the concrete system. If, however, the law is connected with the rise of West Slavic quantity, then its rise is apparently connected with the development of contraction.

4.2 If it is valid that Central Slovak has a number of South Slavisms, then the question immediately arises, whether the rhythmic law is not a matter of certain reflexes of the South Slavic prosodic relationships of that period. At the same time, it is necessary to expect — in regard to the fact that this is a post-jer development, c.f. 3.4 — other contacts than those according to diagram 2. Central Slovak-South Slavic contacts were already weakened; Central Slovak integrated with the remaining Slovak dialects into one language. Here, therefore, the West Slavic system, i.e., the rise of the new quantity, already predominated over certain features from South Slavic prosody. It is obvious that Slovenian dialects still extended farthest north in that period;

the Central Slovak dialect, retreating to the north, could have established contact with them.

4.3 If we seek in the North Slovenian dialects prosodic features analogous to those of Central Slovak, then to the rhythmic law corresponds the principle of secondary stress in certain Carinthian dialects. Thus, e.g., in the Rozanski dialect, trisyllabic oxytones take another stress on the first syllable, which is lengthened, c.f. Ramovš 1952, 17. It is important that only stressed syllables may be long. The author, *ibid.*, notes: ". . . it is not, then, excluded that the secondary stress is old". The Ziljski dialect has similar relationships. In addition, it is remarkable for a number of such features as *dl, tl* preserved almost to the West Slavic extent, the prefix *vy-*, the contraction *moja > má, moje > (mé >) mó* in contrast to uncontracted *mojemu,* lengthening of the type *neséš (< nesèš),* in certain subdialects *g > γ,* etc., cf. *op. cit.,* p. 8 ff. Certain Carinthian and Styrian dialects contravene the rule of intonational opposition, i.e., for both long intonations there is only phonological quantity (cf. *op. cit.* p. 4 *passim*), so that the stressed syllable is only the bearer of quantity.

4.4 There is a very similar situation in the Nový Hrad region of Central Slovak. That is to say, there quantity is tied to stress and the rhythmic law is equally valid, cf. Pauliny 1963, 269. Therefore, the principle is very similar: length is tied to stress; adjacent unstressed syllables must be short. Even the Central Gemer dialect, cf. *ibid.,* can, despite the lack of the rhythmic law, remind one of Slovenian dialects, cf. Ramovš 1952, 8.

4.5 The tying of quantity to stress, as Pauliny 1963, 269, points out, is a remarkable Central Slovak phenomenon which recalls certain South Slavic features. If we assume that there were still Central Slovak contacts with South Slavic even after the fall of the jers, i.e., after the 10th century, then the union of the dominant West Slavic quantity with certain features in Slovenian undoubtedly belongs among the most important objectives of research into these contacts.

CHAPTER XIX

SAMPLE RECONSTRUCTION OF CHANGES IN CONJUGATION FROM PROTO-SLAVIC THROUGH THE HISTORICAL PERIOD OF THE CONTRACTION LANGUAGES

1. INTRODUCTION

1.1 In this chapter we shall not attempt a description of the entire conjugational system; rather, the main objective will be to comprehend the chronological sequence of the changes that were realized here, not merely, of course, those changes that also have a surface character, but also the sequence of certain further underlying changes, such as the integration and disintegration of the individual conjugational types. The subject of our investigation will not be, of course, to describe the formation of the morphological category of contract in conjugation, for that was the goal of XIV/5; rather, it will be the concrete investigation of the results and consequences of contraction for the conjugational system.

1.2 We shall proceed in this case from the system that realized contraction and its consequences most consistently, i.e., from the system of Czech. Differentially, we shall also call attention to certain peculiarities of the other contraction languages. In principle, however, we are dealing with a compact process: whereas on the phonological plane we observe sharp distinctions between the West Slavic and the South Slavic territories (cf. XVIII/2-3), on the morphological plane the whole contraction territory develops in essence uniformly and, what is more, not only in the period of contraction, but also in the realization of the consequences of these differences in conjugation, up to the historical period. That allows this outline to preserve formal and chronological unity, even though in certain later stages it is no longer a question of isoglosses but of concurrent, parallel development arising from correspondences of conditions.

1.3 In this outline we also include the imperfect, which later became a component of the development because in it the coalesced vowel was interpreted as a contract, so that it also functioned as the bearer of the category of contract, XIV/5.5 ff.

2. SOME IMPORTANT FEATURES OF PRECONTRACTION CONJUGATION

2.0 The precontraction conjugational system has all the features of the Proto-Slavic conjugation. We shall here concern ourselves only with those which underwent fundamental changes.

2.1 The root and suffixed verbs form in the present tense a single class of *j*-stems verbs, cf. XIV/5, especially 5.1. The differences are in the infinitive stem: the stem is either of the type *dělati* : *lajati* or of the type *kupovati* : *čuti*, finally of the type *šiti, kryti* :∅ (*prositi* is not a *j*-stem verb). The similarities are only in cases of the type *uměti* : *spěti,* cf. *grějati/grěti,* etc. On this difference see further 3.7.

2.2 The class of *j*-stem verbs belongs to the category of verbs with the present tense marker *e/ǫ*, cf. *nesešь, nesǫtь*. These stand in opposition to *i*-type verbs *prosišь*. This opposition forms the category of "thematic" verbs, which is sharply distinguished from the category of "athematic" verbs in the structure of its forms and in its endings. Only the verb *jьmamь* forms a bridge between them. This system is in principle preserved in East Slavic; deviations from the system in non-contraction languages are connected chiefly with transperipheral and similar processes, cf. III/5.2 and 6.

2.3 The verb *jesmь* agrees in its main features with other verbs of the athematic category. The most important feature of this verb within this category is extreme suppletion, i.e., variability of stem linked with non-paradigmatic variations of stem in a single paradigm: *jes-/s-//by-/bǫd-/* . . .

2.4 In the imperfect tense the original structure disappears even before the rise of contraction. This is a Common-Slavic phenomenon, cf. III/3.2.

3. CHANGES IN THE PHONOLOGICAL STAGE — *neje, lajati*

3.0 It is obvious that the verb *jьmamь* vaulted over the sharp boundary between thematic and athematic verbs. Why, then, is *ně* < *neje* treated as thematic, i.e., as being without an ending in the 3rd pers. sing.?

3.1   In Old Czech *je* is rarer than *jest,* cf. Gebauer 1960, 415, 418; in Old Polish the form *je* is entirely exceptional, cf. Klemensiewicz et al. 1964, 363. Nevertheless, there is, on the contrary, only the form *neně,* i.e., without desinential inflection.

3.2   It is claimed that Slovak *nie som, nie si,* etc. reflect the old contracted forms *nĕsmь* < *nejesmь,* etc., known also in Serbo-Croatian, cf. Stanislav 1958, 513 f. It is precisely in Central Slovak, where these forms are known; with regard to the chronology of their rise, they appear as South Slavisms, cf. XIX/3.4.

The same form exists in Old Church Slavic; here, of course, it is not a question of contraction, but of the coalescence of **ne esmь**, still in the period when the oppositions e : ĕ, o : a had mainly a quantitative character, cf. Horálek 1962, 145. On the contrary, the change, which presupposes contraction length, must have been realized much later, when the contraction languages already had word-initial I, i.e., **jesmь** and, therefore, also **nejesmь.**

3.3   For the rest of West Slavic, represented by the remaining Slovak dialects, Czech, and Polish, we assume only the existence of a form (*neje* >) *nĕ.* There are no examples for the remaining cases, it is here important that Central Slovak does have them; this lack can be explained by morphological conditions and by negative morphological factors.

3.4   The form *neje,* on the other hand, encountered no obstacles, for it had disengaged itself from the paradigm *jesmь . . . jestь . . .* The question remains: How did it arise, i.e., how did it separate itself from this paradigm, when, after all, here there was no model *umĕ* and its ability to condition changes of the type *vĕstь* > *vĕ?*

3.5   It seems that this change *nejestь* > *neje* arose by integration with root verbs of the type *vĕje, laje . . .* which, except for the ending, had the same structure in this form. The similarity of the structures comes into consideration, however, only in the negative form; that form, therefore, could thus be emancipated — it is, after all, a verb with extreme suppletivism, cf. 2.3 — and could, thus emancipated, undergo contraction.

3.6   This hypothesis can also throw some light on the chronology of the loss of the inflectional suffix *-tь* in thematic verbs; in West Slavic the *terminus ante quem* for it is contraction.

3.7   The form *lajati* is not contracted in South Slavic, nor on the West Slavic periphery — in Polish and Lower Sorbian. The reasons are morphological — it is a matter of the distinction between root verbs and suffixed verbs. This points to definite differences between these two categories already in this period. Contraction in the central region we ascribe to more intensive development which, in addition, led to the integration of this type with the types *šiti, kryti, spěti,* etc.

4. CHANGES IN THE MORPHONOLOGICAL, MORPHOLOGICAL, AND MORPHOLOGIZED STAGES

4. These stages represent a principal reversal in the development of conjugation. This system passed into MM almost complete as to contraction.

4.1 In systems in which contraction of the type *lajati* did not occur (cf. 3.7), the type *sějati* as a rule does not contract either. The difference between Polish *łajać : siać* are perhaps of dialectical origin. The remaining languages realize contraction. Thus, in the first the proportion *dělati : lajati, uměti : sějati* is preserved; in the second, however, these root types are integrated into the other root types, cf. 3.7.

4.2 The most substantial change is, however, the rise of the new present tense contraction paradigm, i.e., *uměješь > uměšь* in MF, *dělaješь > děláśь* in M. Thus, these types also come into contact with the type *jьmašь*.

4.3 In MM we assume a change of the type *smьjati sę > sm'áti sę* on the territory where ExD. was *láti, sáti.* Thus was completed the category of contract in conjugation.

5. CHANGES CONNECTED WITH THE FALL OF THE JERS

5.0 J is connected with the fall of the jers. In the area of conjugation this stage had only contrasystemic consequences in the changes *pьjǫ > p'ǫ, pьješь > pěšь* . . . , which were sooner or later nullified. The fall of the jers itself has, however, serious consequences for the morphological plane (noun), rather than for the phonological plane.

5.1 The phonological consequences of the fall of the jers can have an influence on the development of morphology. With the loss of the old intonations, which is connected with the fall of the jers, cf. XVII/2.2-3, any phonetic barrier between the types *uměš, děláš* on the one hand and the type *prosiš* on the other is set aside. This type develops into the contraction paradigm; it has, in this case, the shape *prosíš.*

5.2   With the fall of the jers there is lost the requirement that verbs of the contraction paradigm must have syllabic roots; thus there arise forms like *směš. . . , zráš . . . ,* etc. cf. XVI/1. After contraction and the loss of intonations (cf. 5.1), this is the next step forward the rapprochement of the athematic verbs with the contraction paradigm. On the basis of the corresponding forms of the two systems the old system of endings in the athematic paradigm begins to be replaced by the new system, which has at its disposal not only the contraction paradigm itself, but also the whole thematic conjugation. It is more than likely that the verb *jmáš,* which agrees with the athematic verbs in the 1st pers. sing. and with the contraction paradigm in the other persons, played an important role in the integration of the two systems.

5.3   The verb *jesm,* which cannot, because of its structure, find a partner among the contraction types, becomes isolated.

5.4   After this rapprochement there still remains the difference among the forms of the 1st. pers. sing. *dělaju : dám, jmám; uměju : věm.* The contraction paradigm here shows a structural exception: in contrast to the other forms of the singular, there is here a syllabic ending and it does not have the feature of quantity. This position is so weak that, in contrast to the others, this form, instead of spreading to the athematic verbs, adopts their ending with much more homogenous structure within the paradigm. If we had to express this in terms of morphological contingencies — on this cf. Chapters IX-X — then it would have the following shape:

dělaju > *dělám*	In.	*děláš, dělá . . .*
uměju > *umćm*		*uměš, umě*
	ExD.	*dám, věm . . .*
	ExG.	*děláš : dáš*
		uměš : věš

which is a direct condition, i.e., one with the maximum of morphological factors.

Thus, in the present tense system two subsystems were definitely formed — a finite subsystem, to which belong all forms of the present indicative in this type except the 3rd pers. pl., and a mixed subsystem, to which belong the remaining forms formed from the present tense stem.

5.5   The distribution of this type, where even the 1st pers. sing. belongs to the present tense subsystem, was, in certain languages, gradually extended over the entire conjugation — this refers to Slovak and South Slavic. Elsewhere, in Polish and partially in Sorbian, on the other hand, development stopped at the stage discussed in 5.4, for there were no direct motives for further changes: the ending in *proszę, prošu,* was not so striking, not surpassing the other forms of the singular; the forms of *prosíš* did not have, in fact, ExD.

Czech was also close to this fate; it seems that here only sound changes of the type *uměš* > *umíš* contributed to the rise of the form 1st pers. sing. *prosím.* The penetration of *-m* into the entire conjugation in Slovak has its own particular systemic motivations — in accordance with the rhythmic law there arose such homonymous forms as *píšu : píšu,* 1st pers. sing. : 3rd pers. pl.

6.   A DIAGRAM OF THE DEVELOPMENT

The processes described in this chapter can be summarized as in table 13 (the table represents the development of West Slavic; for the pertinent differences and other peculiarities adduced in this chapter, see the references in the relevant column):

Explanations of symbols:

   Column 2: $a \succ\!\!\prec b$: *a* integrates with *b,* reciprocal
             integration
             $a \succ\!\!\rightarrow b$, $b \leftarrow\!\!\prec a$: *a* integrates into *b,* unilateral
             integration
             $a \leftrightarrow b$: *a* diverges from *b,* disintegration
   Column 3:   U/S: an underlying or surface development
             U: underlying development
             S: surface development
             S$\rightarrow$ U: a surface development whose result
             was later incorporated into the underlying
             system
             U$\rightarrow$ S: a process opposite to: S $\rightarrow$ U
   Column 4:   reference to Chapter XIX

1. Chronology		2. Examples of changes	3. U/S	4. see
absolute	relative			
before 850	before contraction	W. Slavic *nese* (=PS1 *nesetъ*)		3.6
before 850	before contraction	Common Slavic *dělaaše* > *děláše*	S→U	2.4
2nd half of 9th century	P	*kryji* > *krý*, *pьji* > *pí* . . .	S	
2nd half of 10th century	F	1. *neje* > *ně̌* 2. *lajati* > *láti* ⇒ *láti* >→ *kryti*, *spěti* ⇒ *laje* >—< *kryje*, *spěje*	U U	 3.
	MF	1. (*láti* ⇒) *sějati* > *s̓áti* ⇒ *sěje* >—< *laje*, *kryje* 2. *uměje* > *umě̌* ⇒ a. *umě̌* >—< *prosi* b. *umě̌* ↔ *sěje* *umě̌*:*sěje* ⇒ *prosí*:*šije*	U U	4.1 4.2
	M	(*umě̌* ⇒) *dělaje* > *dělá* ⇒ a. *dělá* >—< *umě̌*, *prosi* b. *dělá* ↔ *laje* . . . etc., cf. MF 2. c. *dělá* >—< *jьma*	U	4.2
	MM	(*láti*, *s̓áti* ⇒) *smьjati sę* > *sm̓áti sę* = cf. F 2., MF 1.	U	4.3
	J	*pьjǫ* > *p̓ǫ̌*, *pьješь* > *p̓ěšь*	S	
11th-12th centuries	after loss of jers	*sъmě̌* > *smě̌*, *zьrá* > *z̓rá* ⇒ *smě̌* . . . >—< *věst'* . . . *z̓rá* . . . >—< *dást'* . . . ⇒ *vě̌*, *dá*	U	5.2
13th-14th centuries	beginnings of individual historical languages	*smě̌*, *umě̌* ⇒ *vě̌* ⇒ *vě̌m* <—< *směju*, *uměju* *z̓rá*, *dělá* ⇒ *da* ⇒ *dám* <—< *z̓raju*, *dělaju* *píti* : *šíti*, *krýti*, *láti* ⇒ *p'ú*, *p̓ěš* >→ *šiju*, *šiješ* . . .	U U→S	5.4

TABLE 13

CHAPTER XX

CONCLUSIONS

1. PURPOSE OF SUMMATION

In this concluding chapter we shall not offer a summation of the results of this work as a whole, but only a survey of the problems which directly relate to contraction and which this work attempts to resolve.

2. AN ATTEMPT AT THE RECONCILIATION OF LINGUISTIC AND EXTRALINGUISTIC FACTS

2.0 Even though the subject of our investigation was linguistic facts, there also followed from it connection with certain extralinguistic phenomena.

2.1 From the beginning of our investigation we have worked with the concept of a contraction territory. Even though this is obviously a linguistic concept, we do not separate it from its proper geographic context. We proceed from the basic premise of linguistic geography that territorial continuity is a prerequisite for the spread or expansion of a particular linguistic development.

2.2 This continuum, i.e., the contraction territory, has not only its own external boundary, but also it own internal differentiation. On the basis of the results of contraction we can establish fairly exactly its focus in Czech (perhaps in common with West Slovak); the central region, to which, apart from Sorbian, South Polish, East Slovak, the western part of the Slovenian (and to some extent the Serbo-Croatian) dialects; and the periphery, to which belong Lower Sorbian, North Polish, Central Slovak, a large part of Serbo-Croatian (especially Štokavian) and certain remote Slovenian dialects, cf. III/7, diagram 1. From further investigation it is obvious that intensity of development is realized in direct dependence on nearness to the focus.

2.3 These conclusions and further consequences convincingly demonstrate the contacts of the South Slavic languages with the

West Slavic languages in this period: Slovenian was the immediate neighbor of Czech, whereas Serbo-Croatian, particularly its southern region, was in contact with Central Slovak, cf. XVIII/3.3, diagram 2.

2.4 By further investigation it was possible to distinguish two types and two sources of the fall of the jers — Eastern South Slavic, which, without the support of the system, carries out the process with a lack of consistency, and West Slavic, with its focus in Czech, which thanks to the systemic peculiarities acquired in contraction, viz., the loosening of its tight syllabic structure and the softness correlation of consonants, can carry out this process to an unlimited extent, cf. XVII.

2.5 These conclusions have the following form in extra-linguistic reality: the focus of contraction is the region corresponding to the strong political and cultural concentration on the territory of Great Moravia. That part of the contraction territory that closely surrounded the focus represents the territory under the immediate political and cultural influence of this Great Moravan center. The periphery, on the other hand, was not subject to these immediate influences, but nevertheless it did not remain intact in the face of these processes. Its outer limit can be established such that on West Slavic territory the process spread almost to its farthest boundaries — Polabian it not entirely excluded from this process — while the contact to the East was insufficient for further expansion. West Slavic had much closer contacts with the South; here the periphery extended as far as the Eastern South Slavic border. The Eastern South Slavic region, which, from a linguistic point of view, manifests its activity as one source of the development of the jers, is, to be sure, another old Slavic center. Obviously, the neighboring Serbo-Croatian dialects, located on the periphery of a different influence, could not, primarily transmit contraction changes to this center. On the contrary, in the next period, they take from it the impulse toward the loss of the jers, which then spreads throughout the whole of South Slavic and conflicts with the impulse sent from the West Slavic focus.

2.6 Transperipheral changes, i.e., morphological changes primarily motivated by contraction but realized beyond the boundaries of contraction territory — Eastern South Slavic, Ukrainian — are the consequences of later contacts of non-contraction territory with the periphery. Here it is, of course, already a matter of facts well known from history.

2.7   Contraction is a process in which the West Slavic region adopts the active role of the center of development.

3.   UNDERLYING AND SURFACE CHANGES

3.0   In order to determine the essence of contraction it was necessary to differentiate carefully the underlying system from the surface.

3.1   The surface is the totality of the manifestations of two contradictory properties: manifestations of phenomena are that part of language which is directly accessible to our observation, but which does not reflect or at least does not directly have to reflect the particular object of that observation, the underlying system. In contraction, for example, the rise of the forms *krý, ší,* etc. in the primary stage is purely a superficial process, i.e., of itself it does not mean any change in underlying system, whether in the phonological or in the morphological system. On the contrary, the formation of the morphological category of root presents (e.g. *spěje*) does not have to be accompanied by any immediate change on the surface.

3.2   The surface is, therefore, a formation which conveys external influences to the deep structure. It can act either in conjunction with the system or independently of the system, in which latter case it regularly comes into conflict with it. At the time when some manifestation of surface phenomena that are causing traumatic changes in the underlying system, ceases to be valid, forces come into existence that liquidate these changes or adapt them according to the needs of the system. The comparison of the two sources of the loss of the jers showed us that the system which is not ready to accept a particular change of surface phenomena forcefully defends itself, whereas the system which is able to accept this change and apply it to its own needs realizes it more consistently. Also, primary contraction would not lead to systemic changes if the system did not accept them and did not adapt them to its own requirements.

3.3   Subsequent stages of contraction do not noticeably differ as to surface phenomena from the primary stage; however, it is essential that they be realized as systemic changes. Not only the process, but also the conflicts have a systemic nature — here the phonological and morphological planes conflict. Of course, the basis of the conflict lies in the fact that it does not take place within the synchronic structure but within a differentiated diachronic structure between elements of the old and the new systems. This is why conflicts arise not only between planes, or rather, between the new elements of the one plane and the original elements of the other, but also that there are analogous conflicts within these planes. Often, only the coordination of the progressive intentions of the phonological and the morphological planes helps to assert a new element in the face of the original conservative relationships. The rise of the variant $é$ is an assertion of the interests of the new phonological ($\bar{A} = A^2$) and morphological (the contract in adjectives) principles against the old phonological principle '$(e/ě)$.

4. CONTRACTION AND THE SYSTEM

4.0   Contraction has consequences for both the phonological and the morphological system.

4.1   The conflict between the elements of the old quality and the new quality does not have merely an internal nature, i.e., intrasystemic, but also a territorial nature. The more remote the system is from the focus, the fewer new elements penetrate into the system and the more resistant is the old system. Sometimes the old system resists in a single category, e.g., it will not accept the variant $é$ (cf. Central Slovak, Štokavian) or the contraction paradigm of the type $umě̆$ (cf. North Polish, Nadižski dialect of Slovenian); however, sometimes this resistance has a pan-systemic character.

4.2   This is a question of the basic differences in the phonological consequences of contraction in West Slavic and South Slavic. That is, the South Slavic contract adapts to the original prosodic conditions. In South Slavic there are no other phonological consequences because here parallel changes in the jers are carried out by Bulgaro-Macedonian.

4.3   Contrary to this, in West Slavic the contraction processes led to fundamental changes in the phonological system. The quantity of the contract here was not subordinated to the original prosodic relationships; on the other hand, they were subordinated to the new quantity (it might be possible to seek exceptions in extreme peripheral Kashubian). Consequently, it is precisely here that it is most pertinent to speak of the rise of a new phonological category, the category of contract.

4.4 This new category, however, is not the only consequence of West Slavic contraction in the phonological system. Other new features are formed in the contraction syllables — the loosening of the structure of the syllable and the creation of the softness correlation of consonants (by which is explained the loss of epenthetic *l*). What is important is the interdependence and, at the same time, the obligatoriness of all these features in a common syllable, which attests to the autonomy of the contraction syllable within the old system.

4.5 The morphological system has a much more compact development on the entire contraction territory. The morphological category of contract is created, as is demonstrated by the formation of contraction paradigms standing in opposition to non-contraction paradigms and forms. The adjectival declension, at the same time, is shown to be a pronominal contraction paradigm.

4.6 Some contraction paradigms, pronominal and verbal, develop further over the entire contraction territory. In some peripheral dialects, like Štokavian, the contraction paradigm does not arise in the substantive; in other contraction dialects, it developed only to the extent that they sooner or later suppress the phonological category of contract so that this paradigm loses its independence; therefore, it develops further only in Slovak and Czech. In those West Slavic languages in which quantity was lost, the independence of the pronominal contraction paradigm was weakened, and the adjectival declension integrated with the pronominal.

4.7 Contraction struck deep into the system; the deeper it penetrated, the more intensively it was itself realized.

5. CHRONOLOGY AND THE CONSEQUENCES OF CONTRACTION FOR FURTHER DEVELOPMENT

5.0 In establishing the consequences of contraction for further development, it is necessary first to determine its chronology.

5.1 We attempted to resolve the existing arguments about chronology with a new one. One the basis of developments of the type *sъměješь/směješь* (*sę*) → *směš/směješь* (*sę*) we stated the relevance of the jers to the fate of contraction; contraction, therefore, preceded the fall of the jers. Thus the long-standing argument about a special Central Slovak chronology vanishes.

5.2 After this conclusion we find the answer to why the loss of the jers is realized most intensively on West Slavic territory: it was caused by contraction, which here undermined the integrity of the syllable and created the softness correlation.

5.3 This chronology also strengthens the possibility of the reconstruction of West Slavic quantity and stress and the special problems of the Central Slovak rhythmic law.

5.4 The detailed analysis of contraction also provides further possibilities for the precise phasic description of the individual underlying systems and surface phenomena for a complete relative and partially also an absolute chronology. Here these possibilities are applied to one of the systems, the system of conjugation, which underwent striking changes in the course of contraction and its aftermath.

6. CONCLUSION

Neither this chapter nor the whole work has by any means exhausted the possibilities that the problems of contraction, so little investigated, richly afford. Its investigation has, at the same time, immeasureable importance for understanding the breakup of the Slavic continuum, but chiefly for understanding the system of the whole of the contraction territory and the individual contraction languages whose first independent, partially still pre-historic stage, was so deeply affected by contraction.

REFERENCES

Belić 1962, A. **Istorija srpskohrvatskog jezika**, Belgrade.
  Knj. II, Sv. 1: Reči sa deklinacijom
  Knj. II, Sv. 2: Reči sa konjugacijom
Bernštejn 1961, S. B. **Očerk sravnitel'noj grammatiki slavjanskich jazykov**, Moscow.
Bernštejn 1968, S. B. "Kontrakcija i struktura sloga v slavjanskich jazykov" **Slavjanskoje jazykoznanije**, V. V. Vinogradov et al., eds., Moscow, pp. 19-31.
Bezpalko et al. 1957, O. P. **Istoryčna hramatyka ukrajins'koji movy**, Kiev.
Birala et al. 1957, A. Ja. **Narysy pa historyji belaruskaj movy**, Minsk.
Borkovskij 1963, V. I., Kuznecov, P. S. **Istoričeskaja grammatika russkogo jazyka**, Moscow.
Gebauer, J. **Historická mluvnice jazyka českého** (new edition), Prague.
Gebauer 1963, J. Vol. I. (Phonetics).
Gebauer 1958, J. Vol. III, part 1. (Declension).
Gebauer 1960, J. Vol. III, part 2. (Conjugation).
Georgiev 1958, V. **Issledovanija po sravnitel'no-istoričeskomu jazykoznaniju**, Moscow.
Isačenko 1970, A. V. "East Slavic morphophonemics and the treatment of the jers in Russian: a revision of Havlik's law", IJSLP XIII, pp. 73-124.
Horálek 1962, K. **Úvod do studia slovanských jazyků**, Prague.
Klemensiewicz et al. 1964, Z. J. **Gramatyka historiczna jezyka polskiego**, Warsaw.
Komárek M. **Gebauerovo historické hláskosloví ve světle dalšího bádání** (commentary, appended to Gebauer 1963, p. 753ff.).
Komárek 1962, M. **Historická mluvnice česká**, I. Hláskosloví, Prague.
Krajčovič 1962, R. "O príčinách vzniku západoslovanskej kontrakcie", **Acta Universitatis Carolinae, Slavica Pragensia IV**, Prague, pp. 111-115.
Łoś 1927, J. **Gramatyka polska**, III, Warsaw.
Machek 1957, V. **Etymologický slovník jazyka českého a slovenského**, Prague.
Mańczak 1966, W. "Contraction des voyelles dans les langues slaves", **Anzeiger für slavische Philologie**, Band I, Wiesbaden, pp. 52-58.
Mareš 1965, F. V. **The Origin of the Slavic Phonological System and its Development up to the End of Slavic Language Unity**, Ann Arbor.
Mareš 1956, F. V. "Vznik slovanského fonologického systému a jeho vývoj do konce období slovanské jazykové jednoty", **Slavia XXV**, pp. 443-495.

Mareš 1971, F, V. "Kontrakce vokálů v slovanských jazycích", **Slavia, XL**, pp. 525-536.

Marvan et al. 1963, J. "Základní procesy v lexikalním vývoji českého jazyka", **Československé přednášky pro V. mezinárodní sjezd slavistů v Sofii**, Prague.

Marvan 1964, J. "K některým morfologickým otázkám diftongu ej v obecné češtině v konfrontaci se stavem staročeským". **Listy filologické V**, 87, pp. 76-85.

Mirčev 1963, K. **Istoričeska gramatika na bălgarskija ezik**, Sofia.

Mucke 1891, K. E. **Historische und vergleichende Laut- und Formenlehre der niedersorbischen Sprache**, Leipzig.

Pauliny 1963, E. **Fonologický vývin slovenčiny**, Bratislava.

Ramovš 1952, F. **Morfologija slovenskega jezika**, Ljubljana.

Ramovš 1935, F. **Historična slovnica slovenskega jezika, 7. Dialekti**, Ljubljana.

Shevelov 1964, G. Y. **A Prehistory of Slavic, The Historical Phonology of Common Slavic**, Heidelberg.

Stang 1966, Chr. S. **Vergleichende Grammatik der baltischen Sprachen**, Oslo-Bergen-Tromsö.

Schmalstieg 1971, W. R. "Die Entwicklung der ā-Deklination im Slavischen", **Zeitschrift für slavische Philologie, XXXVI**, pp. 130-146.

Stanislav 1958, J. **Dejiny slovenského jazyka, II, Tvaroslovie**, Bratislava.

Trávníček 1935, F. **Historická mluvnice československá**, Prague.

Trubetzkoy 1922, N. S. "Essai sur la chronologie de certains faits phonétique du slave commun", **Revue des études slaves**, Vol. 2, Paris, pp. 217-234.

Trubetzkoy 1929, N. S. "K voprosu o chronologii stjaženija glasnych v zapadno-slavjanskich jazykach", **Slavia VII**, pp. 815-817.

Vážný 1962, V. **Historická mluvnice česká, II. Skloňování**, Prague.

INDEX OF AUTHORS' NAMES

INDEX OF LANGUAGES

INDEX OF WORDS

The Proto-Slavic forms are used for the entry. For non-Slavic languages see Index of Languages.

For abbreviations of languages see p. 19.

Additional abbreviations: E, N, S, W — East, North, South, West; O, OCS — Old, Old Church Slavonic

Carp — Carpathian, CS — Common Slavic, Čak — Čakavian, Mac — Macedonian, Štok — Štokavian

188

zьrati   "ripen"
  zrá   Tab. 13 (164)
  zrám   Tab. 13 (164)
  zráš   128, 162
  zьrá   Tab. 13 (164)
  zьraješь   129
(žegti)   "burn"
  žьdzi (OCS)   130
žena   "woman"
  —   76, 118

ženě   112
ženǫ   73, 76, 109
ženojǫ   73, 121, 122, 140
žęti   "reap"
  žăna (Bu)   144
  žьnǫ   144
žьrati   "eat"
  žéřeš (OCz)   104
  žeru (OCz)   104